Quarterly Essay

Quarterly Essay is published four times a year by Black Inc., an imprint of Schwartz Publishing Pty Ltd. Publisher: Morry Schwartz.

ISBN 9781760640712 ISSN 1832-0953

Subscriptions – 1 year print & digital (4 issues): $79.95 within Australia incl. GST. Outside Australia $119.95. 2 years print & digital (8 issues): $149.95 within Australia incl. GST. 1 year digital only: $49.95.

Payment may be made by Mastercard or Visa, or by cheque made out to Schwartz Publishing. Payment includes postage and handling.

To subscribe, fill out and post the subscription card or form inside this issue, or subscribe online:

quarterlyessay.com
subscribe@blackincbooks.com
Phone: 61 3 9486 0288

Correspondence should be addressed to:

The Editor, Quarterly Essay
Level 1, 221 Drummond Street
Carlton VIC 3053 Australia
Phone: 61 3 9486 0288 / Fax: 61 3 9011 6106
Email: quarterlyessay@blackincbooks.com

Editor: Chris Feik. Management: Caitlin Yates. Publicity: Anna Lensky. Design: Guy Mirabella. Assistant Editor: Kirstie Innes-Will. Production Coordinator: Marilyn de Castro. Typesetting: Akiko Chan.

Printed in Australia by McPherson's Printing Group. The paper used to produce this book comes from wood grown in sustainable forests.

NET LOSS

The Inner Life in the Digital Age

Sebastian Smee

Every day I spend hours and hours on my phone. I have Instagram, Facebook and Twitter accounts. I have three email addresses. I watch soccer highlights, comedy clips, how-to advice and random music videos on YouTube. I download podcasts, which I listen to while driving, and I'm addicted to Waze and Google Maps. I do all this, and much more besides, without much thought, just a little lingering anxiety.

We are all doing it, aren't we? It has come to feel completely normal. Even when I put my device aside and attach it to a charger, it pulses away in my mind, like the throat of a toad, full of blind, amphibian appetite. Habitually, several times a day, I check certain apps that bring me news from the worlds of sport, politics and art. A goal by Zlatan Ibrahimović. A shark attack off La Perouse. The latest tweet by Donald Trump. A painting by Banksy that self-destructs after it is purchased at auction. All of it more or less extraordinary and tending towards the unthinkable, which is precisely the reason I click on it.

I am aware that using apps, signing up for their services and paying for things online means I am handing out information about myself to people whose motives I can't know. I feel I should be bothered by this, but I'm not, particularly. Any potentially harmful ramifications feel too distant, obscured by weedy thickets of cause-and-effect I can't possibly unravel. I try not to think about what the makers of these apps, the advertisers to whom they sell my data, or the people to whom *they* sell it on, think they know about me by now. But it comes to my mind, I admit, whenever I get an incoming call, usually sometime in the early afternoon, which briefly makes me feel as though I may be in the opening scenes of a David Lynch movie. I answer it, knowing better, but ... well, just in case. A prerecorded female voice starts speaking in Mandarin or Russian or robotic American English. I hang up, mumbling an unnecessary explanation to whomever I might be with.

Ah, I tell myself: they know superficial stuff about me, whoever these people are. They know my phone number and my age. They probably know what sports teams I support, what music I listen to, and where I do the weekly food shop. From all this, they can probably guess (though I try to keep my opinions to myself) how I will vote. But they cannot know my inner life.

*

Wait. "Inner life"? What would that even be? I search through old notebooks and come across a passage I wrote down years ago. It's Anton Chekhov, describing Gurov, the character at the centre of his most famous story, "The Lady with the Dog." "He had two lives," writes Chekhov,

> one open, seen, and known by all who cared to know, full of relative truth and of relative falsehood, exactly like the lives of his friends and acquaintances; and another life running its course in secret. And through some strange, perhaps accidental conjunction of circumstances, everything that was essential, of interest and of value to him, everything that made the kernel of his life, was hidden from other people; and all that was false in him, the sheath in which he hid himself to conceal the truth – such, for instance, as his work in the bank, his discussions at the club ... his presence

> with his wife at anniversary festivities – all that was open. And he judged of others by himself, not believing in what he saw, and always believing that every man had his real, most interesting life under the cover of secrecy and under the cover of night.

There is something almost biblical about Chekhov's passage: its commanding clarity, its plain language, its explanatory force. The imagery here could not be more explicit. In Gurov, Chekhov is saying, and perhaps in all of us, there is an inside and there is an outside. The inside, the "kernel," hidden from other people, is essential, of interest, real. It may be harder to get to know – it runs its course in secret – but in the quest for self-knowledge, it has tremendous prestige. (It is not by accident that we are reading about it in a prestigious work of fiction: our "inner lives" are precisely what we expect to learn about in literature.) The outside, the "sheath," is all relative and, at its worst, false, a sham.

This conception implies a whole philosophy of selfhood, and a whole literature to go with it. There would be no Virginia Woolf, Marcel Proust, James Joyce or Robert Musil; there would be no *Catcher in the Rye*, no Albert Camus, no Christina Stead or Alice Munro without this troubling distinction between a true core and a sham exterior.

I say "troubling" only because there is a sense in the passage that something is not right. What is sham and what is true? That's one problem – one I'm not about to try to solve. The other is more immediate. It's that the distinction between inside and outside, so sharply etched, feels fundamentally worrisome. It is the source, Chekhov seems to be suggesting, of an unknown malaise in Gurov. He is a man divided. There is a pressure building within him, which may be intolerable. There may not be a gun on the wall, but there's no doubt about it: Gurov is headed for trouble.

*

In this essay, I want to dig into this idea that we all have an inner life with its own history of metamorphosis – rich, complex and often obscure, even to ourselves, but essential to who we are. It is a part of us we neglect at our peril. I am interested in it because of my sense that, as we live more and more of our lives online and attached to our phones, and as we are battered and buffeted by all the informational, corporate and political surges of contemporary life, this notion of an elusive but somehow sustaining inner self is eroding. I think this may be a bigger change, with more serious ramifications, than we realise. Once nurtured in secret, protected by norms of discretion or a presumption of mystery, this "inner" self today feels harshly illuminated and remorselessly externalised, and at the same time flattened, constricted and quantified.

The companies shaping our new reality have powerful tools. They promise to connect us on social media; to entertain us on reality TV, YouTube and Facebook; to identify, target and even diagnose us through surveys, questionnaires and tests; to win our votes, enlist our support and market their wares and services. All this is being done. New efficiencies are being found. Meanwhile, the idea of a dark, inner being, silent, inaccessible – the part of us that comes into view while standing by a window at dusk, while walking in the suburbs at midnight or while listening to a melancholy song – has come to seem exotic and unfamiliar, like a rumoured lake in a vast forest, a living body of water which no-one has seen for years. Is this idea of the self, from which whole histories of literature and art have been woven, a mere fiction? Or is it just a stagnant entity, a despised leftover of an exhausted and tattered humanism?

We can no longer assume that it has its own reality. To the extent that it exists at all, it seems to have no place in public discourse. Even in discussions of art, it is ignored, thwarted, factored out. The senses with which we could have grasped, recognised and nurtured it are atrophying. Our children, from a young age, are encouraged to present performative versions of themselves online, and these versions, concocted from who knows what combination of software design, peer pressure and fantasy, appear to take on greater and greater substance in the formation of their characters. They are lonely, it sometimes seems. But the devices pulsing in their pockets or propped near their pillows as they sleep reassure them that they are never far from virtual connections – even if those connections may be fraught in ways beyond their ken. In their constant recourse to these devices, they are only following the example set by the adults around them, who stare at our screens all day, who feel visibly bereft without our phones and the illusion they create of wisdom and connectivity and infinite memory, so that no adorable moment need ever go unphotographed, and no photograph is ever lost. It gets harder, in any case, to be alone with ourselves or to pick up a book; harder still to stay with it.

*

What do I mean by inner life?

Your inner life may be obscure even to yourself. Like freedom, it is hard to define except negatively. It has to do, I assume, with your age and personal history, with the ebb and flow of chemicals inside your brain, and with your body's itches and aches. But also, I would say, with your apprehensions of beauty, your intimations of death, what is going on inside you when you are in love, or when your whole being is in turmoil.

Inner life carries on at a knight's leap remove from opinions and politics, from news headlines and from the tailored ads that appear algorithmically in your inbox. It is obscurely affected by the weather, yes, by the angle of the sun's rays overhead and by shifts in atmospheric pressure. Perhaps also by an early, traumatic experience, the last great book you read, your most recent humiliation, or the last intensely beautiful person you saw in the street. But all this in ways you would struggle ever to put into words.

"Inner life" is not a literal description, it is a metaphor – and in some ways a misleading one. I'm not sure, for instance, that it is, in fact, "inner" – even if we are to use that term figuratively. Just as often it comes into play when we feel ourselves to be in an intensely charged relationship with things, or people, or works of art, that are outside us; when, for instance, we are "wooing" those distant parts of ourselves Alice Munro once wrote about: "I seemed to be often looking for a place to hide," confessed the narrator in one of her stories – "sometimes from the children but more often from the jobs to be done and the phone ringing and the sociability of the neighborhood. I wanted to hide so that I could get busy at my real work, which was a sort of wooing of distant parts of myself." Inner life is our "real work." Those distant parts, which Munro's narrator wants to woo, are like the pressure she needs to bring back her self-definition, her sense of reality.

The obscurity and unknowability of our inner selves is a nuisance, perhaps even a threat, to the social media companies and their software developers who frame and direct so much of our daily attention. It impedes their software's ability to get to know us, and thus our ability to use the software. And yet, of course, we want to use the software (the software knows how to make us want it). So we do what we must. We make available to the software a version of ourselves it can more easily work with. We *reduce* ourselves in order for it to fit. "We know," as Zadie Smith wrote when *The Social Network* came out, "that having two thousand Facebook friends is not what it looks like. We know that we are using the software to behave in a certain, superficial way toward others ... But do we know, are we alert to, what the software is doing to us? Is it possible that what is communicated between people online 'eventually becomes their truth'?"

I don't claim to know the answer to Smith's questions. But I am interested in the process of adaptation, or reduction, because there is a sense in which we are being humiliated by it. And betrayed. Betrayed by corporations, data sets, statistical analyses and the algorithms that would presume to know us. But betrayed, too, by ourselves – by our willingness, what can often seem our eagerness, to make ourselves smaller.

Is it a pity? If you believe that we are larger, more mysterious, deeper, more multivalent and less easily exploited than the software designers would like us to be, then yes, it is a pity – if only because when we ramble through strange cities at night; when we walk in the shadows of mountains or along deserted beaches; when we watch our children sing in a choir or hum and mutter themselves to sleep; when we look into an animal's eyes after putting down our phones; or when we stand before a painting of a boy made 500 years ago, it does seem, does it not, that we are, all of us, harder to account for than the current orthodoxy would have it?

*

I was talking with a friend of mine recently – he lives in London, he works in the global gas trade. He thinks we are all basically just algorithms – by which I think he means that we are like constantly developing sets of instructions carrying out the various operations and interactions required to keep us alive and in good health and getting what we want; or like problems to be solved by calculation. We are very sophisticated algorithms, to be sure (although god help us, look how dumb we can be!). But really, says my friend, that's all we are. Or at least, he might say, that's the most useful and least deluded way to understand ourselves.

I know where he is coming from. Pressed to offer an account of how things work, I am basically a materialist myself, and content to acknowledge (although I know little about it) that mathematical calculation seems to underlie much of material reality. For my friend, things work by cause and effect. If this and this, then this, that and the other. And so on. Yes, sure, it's a problem when we don't know this and this. You always have to acknowledge and try to account for what Donald Rumsfeld astutely called the "known unknowns" and the "unknown unknowns." But that's the way it goes, and the good news is, we know more than we ever did. We are animals with big brains on planet earth. We live in societies, we organise ourselves according to our best advantage. Things are always – but *always* – going wrong. Yet the algorithms adjust. Hopefully things get better. If they don't, too bad, we all die anyway. And that's actually part of the algorithm: death is just "not life," another all-but-arbitrary term in the whole big equation.

Lacking conviction in any alternative explanation, this is actually, I admit, pretty close to how I see things too. We would all save ourselves a lot of trouble, I tend to think, if we could only remember that we are, in fact, animals on a planet in the middle of a universe we only dimly understand; that free will is at best a useful fiction; that we and everything else living will die; and that all things, both dead and alive, are in constant flux.

And yet I am bored already.

What's more, I'll be honest, I don't particularly *feel* like an algorithm. I stare at my bookshelf, or at a painting in a gallery, or I wander through the streets that surround where I live, and I struggle to reconcile the sentences inside the books, or the 100-year-old tree I love, its leaves trembling in the urban gloaming, or the painting in the local museum I always return to, with the idea that we are all basically algorithms. It is difficult. Is the resistance I feel explained by the fact that I am too wedded to old, sentimental, deluded ways of seeing, as represented by these books, that old idea of "nature," those paintings?

My friend would probably say so. He is extremely congenial. But he has no time, frankly, for airy-fairy nonsense. He has a global economy to supply with gas, rational calculations to make. Also, he needs to get to the gym before the day is out and to organise a present for his son's birthday. That last will be hard. His wife may help. She is a banker, who helps investors back the right renewable energy companies. Things are changing so quickly now, she tells me; the whole energy economy is being dramatically overhauled. To charge my phone, for instance, I'll soon have a little solar panel on the back of the device so that I can just put it panel-side up on a table to charge. Problem solved. Problems *are* being solved. A few years ago, she managed investments in the global food industry and its various supply chains. When she talked about her work back then, she reminded me of what I secretly knew but didn't and still don't want to admit: that when we go to the supermarket we are the worst kind of dilettantes. We rarely think about where our neatly packaged meat and gorgeously stacked, mist-sprayed vegetables come from. We don't want to.

She knows, however. On a work trip to Kenya, on behalf of investors, she once visited a farm where French beans are grown, prepared and packaged for a supermarket chain in the United Kingdom. A third of the workers there, and many of their children, had AIDS. So the company that ran the farm did the rational thing: it built a hospital at the farm and set up strict protocols (algorithms, really) for what to do when, as happens all the time, a worker with AIDS cuts herself while topping and tailing the beans.

That was one issue. Another was that none of the workers at the farm had bank accounts. So the company had a problem to solve. Gangs who knew when payday was would wait for the buses to unload the workers back in their village after their shift. The gangs would mug them and take their money. So to lower the likelihood of those terrible scenes, the company decided to pay them not weekly or monthly but irregularly, unpredictably.

These were, said my friend, the realities – problems for the farm management and the supermarket chain to solve, and for its investors to back with funding, so that, down the line, profits would be made. If *this* (workers and their children have AIDS), then *this* (onsite hospital, sterilisation protocols). If *this* (no bank accounts) and *this* (poverty, gangs, theft), then *this* (unpredictable paydays). Straightforward. This is the stuff that people with real responsibilities – as opposed to art critics and dilettantes – have to deal with. Philosophise all you like. It won't change anything.

Given the gravity and sheer scope of the things they are dealing with, my friends have no time for sentimentality. They admire art, literature, dance and classical music – they go to concerts (she trained as a classical musician) and to the ballet, and they will occasionally visit museums – but they certainly have no time for proposing elaborate solutions to things that are not, indisputably, problems. I admire them more than I can say. They are instinctively generous people. They are funny and forthright. But of course, they are certain types. (The world does consist of types – there's no getting around it.) They are brisk-minded, rational – which makes them ideally suited to (algorithmic) problem-solving. I am a different type – arty, I suppose (although I cringe and squirm to admit it) – which to them represents certain admirable or enviable things but is ultimately perhaps a bit risible. I don't disagree.

But inevitably, as an arty type, I see things differently. I think they are missing something. But what?

What's interesting to me about the passage from "The Lady with the Dog" is that Chekhov doesn't try to get at what this supposedly essential inner life might be. He is, after all, a fiction writer – he knows when to keep things open and enigmatic; how to smudge the lines a little at the corners of the mouth and the eyes, as Leonardo did when painting Lisa Gherardini. Chekhov only really gets at what this interior kernel *isn't*, and what it feels like, consequently, to have two lives, one apparently at odds with the other. So perhaps we need, if we want to get a purchase on "inner life," to think more laterally. We could find a way to define it negatively, perhaps – to see what the human personality looks like when there is no inner life, when everything is externalised.

Two young American artists, Ryan Trecartin and Lizzie Fitch, have earned deserved acclaim for giving us the best picture to date of what this looks like. Seeing their work, which is hilarious, ingenious, frantic and funny, an older person might think they are describing a nightmare, futuristic scenario. If you have a teenage daughter you know for certain that their work is describing realities that already exist.

Trecartin, who teamed up with Fitch at art school, was born in Texas. He grew up in Ohio in the 1980s and '90s. Popular in school, he had, by his own account, a joyful childhood, loving parents. But he was acquainted early on with the tension that can exist between the self we present and the one we keep hidden – between inner and outer life. Although he knew he was gay, he did not feel he could tell his parents. He lived, too, in fear of AIDS. When he was seventeen, his mother gave him a Sony Handycam. Inspired by the movie *The Blair Witch Project*, which had just come out, he used a night-vision lens to film a week-long ritualised "war" between the juniors and seniors at his high school. It involved vandalism, binge drinking, partying and run-ins with the police. The footage he took is blurry and filled with menace (one thinks not only of *Blair Witch* but of nature documentaries showing lions and hyenas terrorising the savannah at night).

We see high schoolers smashing in mailboxes with baseball bats and saying – as high schoolers do – abrupt, emphatic things, without concern for how their statements relate to reality, or to any preceding statements.

This – the emphatic non-sequitur – has become a kind of structural principle underlying Trecartin's videos. "I always throw up and then I keep going," says one male student in *Junior War*. "It's fun that way. I don't want to be around people making fun of me."

"Everyone's gotta bring it down a level right now," says another.

"They didn't have probable cause to fuckin' pull us over!" asserts a girl, while another can be heard saying: "She wasn't drunk, she just had sex on the toilet."

Trecartin's first introduction to contemporary art came when a teacher showed him photographs by Cindy Sherman – an artist whose brilliant adoptions of different guises enact a drama of the self as manifold yet always teetering on the edge of breakdown. These made a big impression. He later attended Rhode Island School of Design, where he met Fitch, a fellow student. They began collaborating. Over the past two decades, using a troupe of performers, hyperkinetic editing and hilarious, often improvised scripts that waver in tone between drag burlesque, the poetry of John Ashbery and purest frat-party inanity, they have made one brilliant film after another.

Their characters are like literal incarnations of the avatars and clones of internet culture, the "selves" who spew vitriol, humour and random assertion, and unspool across YouTube comment threads and social media. The characters' outfits and make-up are egregiously crass, their voices often sped up to helium pitch or dripping in caramelised Southernness. Their statements tilt towards teenage vapidity: "I was really sad because they forgot to assign me a sitter and I waived all my rights on the accident," says a girl in CENTER JENNY. Or, in another exchange that kicks off a ritual too involved to explain:

> "Everyone put their phones in the middle of the room and let's get started."
>
> "I'm just waiting for my boyfriend to text me first."

"Your soul is no match for this shit."

"If you don't have the phone in the circle, no-one's going to be able to fetch you if you generate too much content."

This stuff – it's not Chekhov – comes thick and fast. Towards the end of CENTER JENNY, a frighteningly confident monologist articulates what could easily double as subliminal messaging on *Keeping Up with the Kardashians*:

> I might be some privileged bitch, but I'm going to fuck you up, because I'm a privileged bitch that knows how to do that shit. And I might throw a fucking brick in your face, cos you don't know, we might be friends, we might not, but whatever, I'm the only one that knows.

What are these hopped-up, hectic videos telling us? It would be short-sighted to claim that they are "about" social media and new technologies. But they are, as Trecartin has said, about how these new technologies and the frames they create are affecting the way all of us, teenagers and adults alike, relate to the world, how we conceive of ourselves and how we communicate with one another. Their manic intensity and comic energy exaggerate reality, to be sure (even reality as it's found online). But just as the clashing colours, angular figures and compressed space in German expressionist paintings of the 1920s emphasised schizophrenic cleavages in German society, Fitch and Trecartin are making work that speaks to who we are right now.

To begin with, they put the lie to the idea that identity – on the internet or indeed anywhere else – is or ever could be stable. The self, they show, can no longer realistically be compared to a house, with foundations, an inside and an outside; nor is it rational, like the decision tree of an algorithm. Personality, they suggest, is more like a yacht in an ocean race that has run into a cyclone: unmoored, anarchic, lurching hither and thither, at the mercy of massive outside forces.

But, you know, it's also fun! Watching Trecartin and Fitch's videos, you can't help but laugh. They demonstrate that there is an ecstatic freedom, perhaps even a necessary liberation, in giving oneself over to the joy of performance – of turning identity (as it's conventionally understood) inside out and, like a cubist portrait having a messy night out on the town, letting it be what it wants to be: performative, splintered, amoral and unencumbered by logic. All of us – Chekhov's Gurov included – might be in a better place, they imply, if we had this kind of repertoire of selves to draw on, rather than existing in an old-fashioned, bifurcated state, with an inner, secret self and an outer, social one.

But that's not quite the end of it. Other truths emerge from these films like bats from a cave at night. Watching them is like being at a party where everyone is trying to be heard at once. Which is to say, it's like being on Instagram or Twitter. The jagged, incoherent feeling they create in the viewer comes from the sense – intensely familiar to teenagers, but perhaps also, increasingly, to journalists, politicians, doctors and schoolteachers (people who could once command an audience) – that no one is listening. The films propose that no one *need* listen. We are no longer talking about traditional communication. Rather, we are dealing with what the curator Massimiliano Gioni has called a "melodrama of solipsism."

In another of their works, "I-Be Area," Trecartin plays a clone trying to find his independent identity. In writing the script, he explained, he worked from the premise that people are defined by the relationships they maintain with others. "You are your area, rather than you are yourself," Trecartin told Calvin Tomkins. "If someone describes you, that description becomes a part of your area, whether you like it or not." He went further: "We're becoming more flexible and negotiating what the self can be, and the different places the self can exist. It's not just being in a physical space anymore."

*

What is a "self"?

Trecartin's idea of it is one possible answer. Chekhov's is another. But there are countless alternatives. In fact, the question of what constitutes a self has never been less settled than it is at present.

It may be that the idea of the self is an illusion – an artificial construct, a trick of the brain as it tries to organise and cope with reality. But let's assume for now that it is real (and acknowledge that even an artificial construct has a kind of reality). The self could be seen in various ways, not all of them mutually exclusive.

Most straightforwardly, it could be the product of what we know (and hope to find out) of the brain's neurochemistry and neurophysiology. We are advancing quickly in these areas, where the assumption is that everything is made up of chemicals and can be described as physical processes, and that in this sense the brain is not fundamentally different to other phenomena (which are also made up of chemicals and describable as processes); nor is it ultimately *separate* from those outside chemicals and processes.

Others insist that the self is a unique thing. It is rooted in the material world, yes, but it has its own deep, existential coherence. It is a thing with its own impermeable outline. From there, it's a big step, but only a step, to conceiving of the self as a new force in the world, a thing not, in fact, reducible to chemical, physical or informational properties. What we call consciousness – surely central to how we conceive of the self – could exist apart from material reality, on an independent level, as what used to be called a "soul." This soul-like self may arise on its own, be formed by a deity, or derive from an all-pervasive cosmic consciousness.

But then again, the self might not be quite so special. It could instead be described as, for instance, a complex array of properties and relationships that may one day be reproducible outside of our given biology, by a process like uploading.

And on it goes. I'm more or less agnostic on all this. In a way, each of these conceptions is helpful to the extent that it has explanatory force. Like the theory of light as either a wave or a particle, each can be cherrypicked according to its usefulness to the question at hand. To me, for instance, the view of the diffused self as a product of social life makes considerable sense, if only because how we think of ourselves on an everyday level is so heavily determined by how we communicate and are treated by others. To my children, I am a father. To my parents, a son. To my wife, a husband. And to my sister, a brother. Heavy, fraught words, all of them. There are also friends, colleagues, acquaintances, people I know of but am yet to meet, and vice versa. Aren't these the relationships that determine my sense of my own self?

Perhaps. But there is surely more to it. We are told we are social creatures, and god knows it's true. But we don't have to be introverts to grasp how disorienting and exhausting – and ultimately deforming of who we feel ourselves to be – all this continuous *relating* to other people can be.

So there's the rest of the world to take into account – or at least the parts of it with which we interact. What ideas of the self do they posit? Do they liberate us or ensnare us further?

To corporations, I know, I am a consumer, from which many assumptions flow. In fact, this designation – "consumer" – may be the single biggest determining factor in contemporary views of the self. But let's say I am unsatisfied with being a mere consumer. In fact, let's say that not only my status as a consumer but my job description, my education, my family background, my politics and my nationality are all only partially, and perhaps peripherally, related to whom I feel myself to be. What sort of a thing am I?

I might choose, out of curiosity and a quest for self-knowledge, to sit a personality test. Perhaps the famous Myers–Briggs test. From this, I might learn that I am another kind of thing: a "type" indicated by a sequence of four letters, each sequence corresponding to one of sixteen detailed personality sketches. Architect. Advocate. Logistician. Virtuoso. Commander. Executive. Entrepreneur. And so on. Corporations love these tests: they use them both on the employment and HR side and on the business side, to target consumers.

But I wanted to get away from the corporate view! I could turn, I suppose, to astrology, which is always good fun, and has an only slightly less evidence-based way of categorising the self. (I am a classic Libran, you probably already picked it.) But let's face it, someone with psychiatric training would scoff at this.

So perhaps I need a diagnosis? To a psychiatrist, I am presumably a quite different order of thing, more complex than the Myers–Briggs folks or the star charts would have it, something requiring its own scientific-sounding nomenclature. The jargon employed will depend, of course, on the sort of training the psychiatrist – or psychologist or psychoanalyst – has had. But what if my self stays mute, failing to answer to any of the thousands of conditions, each with its own checklist of symptoms, described in the fifth *Diagnostic and Statistical Manual of Mental Disorders?*

Where else, around me, do I find ideas of what it is to be a self, formed and acted upon? On social media, of course. On Instagram. On Twitter. On Facebook.

On Facebook, I am a photo with a feed, friends, a timeline, memories, and quantities of likes and comments. Or at least, that is how I am presented to other people using the platform. To Mark Zuckerberg and the advertisers he sells to, I am, to be sure, another kind of thing. And to the director of a political campaign, an activist or some other kind of social engineer who may be using information harvested by Facebook, I am a slightly different but related kind of thing: the centre of a complex Venn diagram of overlapping identity and demographic categories. But in any case, I have suddenly become a thing that can be – is constantly being – fed into an algorithm.

*

Let me briefly return here to Trecartin and Fitch. What their work shows us, I think, is a world in which the self can be any number of things. They particularly want to express human personality as it manifests itself online, in this no-longer-physical place, this flexible, borderless state of ongoing negotiation.

After watching a lot of their films, you may feel, as I did, a rising panic. Increasingly, their characters come to resemble deranged puppets. The more you look, the less euphoric, funny and free they seem and the more they appear to be subjected to various kinds of control – the control exerted by peer pressure, certainly, but also by deeper, more structural and perhaps sinister forms of power that are never made visible. "The human era went like that, like a sweatshirt on a camp fire," says Mark Trade, the subject and star of Fitch and Trecartin's eponymous film. The characters' sloppy make-up suggests forms of camp, but also a kind of haste, forced on the characters by a capricious, unknown authority. Their behaviour has both pathos and manic intensity. All of which turns the films' initial pervasive hilarity into something stressful, arbitrary and unrelenting. This has to do, you begin to feel, with things deep down in the recesses of the self being forced to the surface.

"This is the first level," says the black girl with the red and pink hair at the beginning of Trecartin and Fitch's "Item Falls." She is talking to the camera. "There are no names here. I am super simple. Audition for me now. I wanna see you audition … *right now*."

In interview, Trecartin has described his characters as "lost." Their "agency," he said, has been "stripped from them, so they're actually conforming to stereotypes to try to use the fact of being stuck or oppressed or abused as a recreational space, a game."

A key idea followed from this: "If we ever do evolve past all the social constructs that we've put on ourselves," he said, "I would imagine that there might be a moment in time where people would indulge in very limited realities because it's fun. It becomes a therapeutic recreational game or space."

Artists make art. When they speak they get to make huge generalisations, fanciful speculations, unsupported by evidence. They tend not to begin sentences with phrases like "Studies show … " But they do have curious insights! And as a diagnosis of the Zeitgeist, Trecartin's notion – that we may be seduced into indulging "in very limited realities," both because it is fun and because it might feel therapeutic – feels intuitively true to me. It also chimes with Zadie Smith's claim that we tend to "reduce" ourselves in order to "fit" the software designed by social media companies, and proposes an answer to the question of why we might be willing to do this.

It is a casual-sounding insight with profound implications. These implications extend even to the body politic. How else to see America's election of a narcissistic reality TV star and con man to the presidency than as a decision to indulge en masse "in a very limited reality"? Trump's ascendancy could be seen as a product of the desire, in the face of ungraspable complexity, for "a therapeutic recreational game or space," a more "limited reality." After a president who had a complicated inner life, who was forever wary of the dangers of unilateral action, who understood, perhaps to a fault, the limits of power and the deep difficulty of effecting change, how like a longed-for massage for the mind to elect a man so narrow, hollow and limited, and, because of that, so confident, charismatic and decisive: "You're fired!" "Lock her up!" "Build the wall!" "Fake news!"

Social media, which is at the centre of this newly limited reality, has changed the dynamic.

At the centre of the story of social media is Facebook, a company which has a user base "that has no precedent," as Evan Osnos recently wrote in *The New Yorker*, "in the history of American enterprise." No fewer than 2.2 billion people log into Facebook at least once a month: that is about a third, as Osnos points out, of all living human beings.

Facebook is also, as the British author John Lanchester wrote, "the biggest surveillance-based enterprise in the history of mankind." It knows, he said, "far, far more about you than the most intrusive government has ever known about its citizens" – although you can be sure that governments everywhere are learning from its methods. Facebook puts this knowledge in the service of its business model, which is to earn advertising revenue – more ad revenue each year than the combined ad revenue of all of America's newspapers. Advertisers like Facebook not only for its almost unimaginably vast reach, but for its ability to "microtarget" ads at users with particular susceptibilities.

Facebook and some other social media platforms also have the power – some would say the responsibility, given the Pandora's box they have opened – to engage in social engineering. Much has been written about the way "bad actors" used Facebook's potential and "psychographic" techniques to affect voting in the 2016 US elections by spreading lies and inciting animus. The Trump campaign accepted an offer from Facebook – an offer also extended to the Clinton campaign (which declined) – to embed Facebook employees inside the campaign organisation who could help craft its messages. Separately, Facebook disclosed that Russian operatives had published about 80,000 posts on Facebook, reaching 126 million Americans.

Measuring the effect of these different forms of attempted persuasion is nearly impossible – although Kathleen Hall Jamieson, a 72-year-old professor of communications at the University of Pennsylvania, has just published *Cyberwar: How Russian Hackers and Trolls Helped Elect a President – What*

We Don't, Can't, and Do Know, in which she makes the case, based on rigorous research, that Russian interference did indeed change the election result. In any case, according to the Trump campaign's digital director, "without Facebook, we wouldn't have won."

Beyond politics, there is plenty to discover about the effect Facebook use may be having, more generally, on wellbeing. The most trustworthy studies, such as one published in the *American Journal of Epidemiology*, find that use of Facebook correlates with diminished wellbeing, both physical and mental. Troubling commentaries have come from within Facebook itself. Osnos's *New Yorker* article quoted Sean Parker, the company's first president, saying "God only knows what [social media is] doing to our children's brains." Chamath Palihapitiya, the former vice-president of user growth at Facebook, was more emphatic: "The short-term, dopamine-driven feedback loops that we have created are destroying how society works. No civil discourse, no cooperation, misinformation, mistruth." Of his own role, he professed to feeling "tremendous guilt," and of his children he said: "They're not allowed to use that shit."

*

The most important question around the use of social media for many people concerns privacy. Way back in 1999, Scott McNealy, the founder and CEO of Sun Microsystems, said: "You have zero privacy … get over it." The statement's abruptness was no longer so shocking in 2010, when Mark Zuckerberg expressed a similar opinion. By then an acceptance of the necessary and possibly even salutary erosion of privacy prevailed in Silicon Valley. That's surely in part because tremendous wealth was being made off the back of the new attitude. As a social norm, privacy had "evolved," said Zuckerberg, because "people [had] really gotten comfortable not only sharing more information and different kinds, but more openly and with more people."

But the degree of comfort people feel tends to depend on how the proposition is framed. When, for instance, users of social media are told that the company running the platform has the right to unlimited, unspecified use of all their photographs of their children and family and loved ones, and when they are told about the possible implications of this as facial recognition technology in artificial intelligence is introduced, they may take a different view. In the meantime, it is hard to resist a kind of passivity or inertia. Until the random afternoon phone call from the Russian bot turns into an actual Russian agent smiling in my living room, I will accept almost anything.

A crucial debate continues to churn around privacy and surveillance, in part because technology continues to leapfrog the law. Security cameras, Doppler radar, licence plate readers, stingrays (devices that mimic mobile-phone towers in order to intercept calls), drones, stingrays mounted on drones, facial recognition and surveillance from the sky are increasingly ubiquitous. In America, where I have lived for ten years, despite the precedent of Supreme Court justices stating that "the right to be let alone is … the beginning of all freedom," US law doesn't know how to keep up. According to Sue Halpern, writing in *The New York Review of Books*, "facial images of more than half the American population already reside in various government databases, collected from such benign activities as renewing a driver's license or reentering the country from a trip abroad." Halpern describes "a new, comprehensive DHS [Department of Homeland Security] database that will include, in addition to facial images … fingerprints, iris scans, DNA data, descriptions of physical anomalies (scars, tattoos), and maps of individuals' affiliations and relationships culled from social media. The DHS will share this database with local and state law enforcement departments, other federal agencies, and certain foreign governments." Other countries, including Australia, are heading the same way, although some European countries are fighting back.

So it is clearly a mistake to think that if you have nothing to hide you have nothing to fear, and that privacy therefore needn't concern you. The kinds of control made possible by a society in which privacy doesn't exist may have nothing to do with your own virtue or harmlessness.

That's because power abhors a vacuum. Unless checked, it will find ways to exert itself. Facebook's facial recognition software can identify you in group photographs. The company also tracks your movements elsewhere on the internet. It wants to fill in the already detailed picture it has, so it buys information about you from data brokers who, in the United States, collect it from pay stubs, store loyalty cards, pharmacy records, voter registrations and motor vehicle information, as well as foreclosure declarations and business registrations. With the profile it builds of each user, Facebook can tailor ads to sell us stuff we want, or can be made to want. But the profile itself is also a commodity which the company sells to advertisers for a great deal of money.

And not just advertisers. Once people's identities are turned into commodities in this way, many different organisations might feel motivated to acquire them. Cambridge Analytica, for example – a political data firm funded by Stephen Bannon, Donald Trump's former chief strategist, and Robert Mercer, a wealthy Republican donor, and hired by Trump's election campaign – appropriated at least 87 million Facebook user profiles. Facebook also sold these profiles to hundreds of other apps. Ignoring users' choices to deny permission to share their personal information, the company shared this information with more than fifty device makers, including Apple, Microsoft, Amazon and Huawei, the Chinese telecommunications company deemed by US intelligence to be a security threat.

Facebook is, of course, far from alone in these practices, as Halpern points out. American mobile-phone network providers allow a company called LocationSmart access to users' real-time locations; LocationSmart sells this information to other companies. Meanwhile, despite promising in 2017 to cease reading its users' emails, Google allows third parties to do so.

*

It has to be concerning that so much information about individual citizens is being harvested and sold in this way. But how accurate are the profiles companies like Facebook build up about us? How much do they really know about us?

A lot – and then, perhaps, not so very much. Specialist companies are already trying to use algorithms to get beyond likes and clicks to predict more subtle and holistic things like happiness, intelligence and political orientation, with the aim, again, of selling the insights. But depending so heavily on data is reductive, for the simple and almost too obvious reason that it leaves out that which cannot be quantified. If, for instance, people who have good credit scores tend to be good employees, that doesn't mean there is a quantifiable connection between the two that can reliably be used to predict job performance. How, in any case, are you even going to define "good job performance," much less quantify it? Algorithms dealing with big and disparate data sets can see patterns where they couldn't previously be detected, which has proved incredibly useful in business, medicine and elsewhere. But algorithms still struggle to cope with the messiness and idiosyncrasy that inhere in individual human beings.

Can we protect ourselves from corporate incursions into our private life by telling ourselves that we have some hidden, impregnable inner life to which the algorithms can never gain access? Is this even realistic? It's very hard to say. One thing we do know is that individual reality is beyond quantification. And cause and effect are always more complex than we like to think. That's in part because perception itself is almost infinitely fluid.

*

An artist who grasped this, with profound consequences for the history of art, was Paul Cézanne. Students of art history know that it is impossible to imagine the cubism of Braque and Picasso, Matisse's experiments in the relativity of colour, or ultimately the abstraction of Kandinsky, Mondrian and Malevich without Cézanne's powerful precedent. What was his insight?

He did a lot of staring at nature, at the landscape around him, and at certain people he wanted to paint. In a 1906 letter to his son, he wrote:

> Here, on the river bank, there are so many motifs, the same object seen from another angle offers a subject of the most compelling interest and so varied that I believe I could work away for months without changing position but just by leaning a little to the right and then a little to the left.

Cézanne was a notorious grouch. But like a Zen adept, he tried to let go of the idea that one thing is more important than another. That logic is easy enough, perhaps, to apply to landscapes. But it's hard to achieve in portraits, where our inherited notion of what constitutes a self dictates that a subject's eyes should be more important than her face, her face more important than her body, and her body more important than the background.

In place of such hierarchies, there is a warp and weft to Cézanne's portraits. In front of "Madame Cézanne in a Red Armchair," a painting which the poet Rainer Maria Rilke claimed to have memorised "digit by digit" until he could feel it even in his sleep, it's hard to be sure which brushstroke is in front and which behind, and impossible to say which part is more important. Cézanne couldn't adjust one part of his paintings without attending to – and altering – the other parts. The process involved duelling loyalties: to the subject, in all its variability; and at the same time to the canvas, in all its variability. The circumstances kept changing, and with it so did the pictures – each one an intricate weaving together of separate little parcels of attention. Life, "Madame Cézanne" announces, is not hierarchical, like a newspaper article, or linear, like an algorithm. It is fluid and multifaceted, like a rippling mosaic. Instead of cause and effect, there are only clusters of interlocking circumstances which mysteriously give rise to new circumstances. It is just painting we are talking about. But it is also an expression of one artist's perception of truth. And it is hard to imagine any algorithm substituting for this kind of responsive, embodied attention.

*

But people are trying. In today's economy, attention has been transformed ever more ruthlessly into a commodity. The battle for it is fierce. On the internet, as on free-to-air television in the past, people get things for "free" in exchange for letting their attention be taken up by various forms of advertising. Advertisers build off tiny parcels of "captured attention."

In the case of Facebook, the most urgent, incessant question, according to Sean Parker, was: "How do we consume as much of your time and conscious attention as possible?" The answers to this question, he said, were arrived at by deliberately "exploit[ing] a vulnerability in human psychology." "Facebook and Snapchat, in their design features," explained Tristan Harris, a former design ethicist at Google, "are persuading a teenager to wake up and see photo after photo after photo of their friends having fun without them, even if it makes them feel worse." Harris, who is quoted in Osnos's *New Yorker* article, described Facebook's platform as a "persuasive technology" – a tool that acts on the user rather than remaining passively in the user's service. Winning our attention, for app developers, is like putting one's foot between the door and the door frame. It is a first, crucial step in an ongoing battle to expand the amount of attention you give.

Some argue the problem is not so much that attention has been turned into a commodity but that it is undervalued. But perhaps the deeper issue transcends valuation; perhaps it is that attention – this phenomenon which philosophers and poets have linked with love, and prayer; which sages have championed as the key to our sense of identification with the world, our wellbeing and even to forms of transcendence – is being commodified to such a thoroughgoing extent in the first place.

*

Understanding the commercial forces behind social media platforms and other digital technologies at least allows us to grasp the motives at play in the competition for our attention. It also helps us see that these seemingly neutral platforms embody particular philosophies, or attitudes to life. As the software becomes ubiquitous, these philosophies become naturalised with astonishing speed. (How long ago was Instagram launched? Eight years. The platform now has 800 million users.)

Facebook (which owns Instagram) embodies an attitude to life that is, when compared to other possibilities, very reductive. Its premise is that we, its users, are actionable areas of self-description and description by others, for the most part photographic and verbal. Responses to these descriptions – in the forms of likes, shares, comments and the whole system of "friending" – can be quantified, aggregated and fed through algorithms, creating a feedback loop for users, but more importantly, a form of sophisticated market research. The whole set-up sounds complicated, in one way. But in fact, its assumptions about who we are and how we relate to one another are cartoonishly simple.

There are huge upsides to Facebook and other social media. Zuckerberg and Facebook's PR team are not wrong when they point to the meaningful connections Facebook makes possible, and the many benefits that flow from these connections. They are real. They create real communities, which often lead to real benefits, and they should not be underestimated. It is hard to imagine the #MeToo movement, for instance, without the connections – the sharing of stories of trauma and the support for that sharing – made possible by social media. The big companies that harness the internet have made the world more connected, more convenient and, in many cases, more efficient. They've made it both easier to measure things and easier to market them. And they've made it easier to get help. All this is massively significant.

But the new dispensation we live under has also accelerated a trend we were seeing before its invention. It is making us more distracted. And it is making the world more open to distortion and exploitation. More disembodied. And somehow less real. It is forcing us to reduce ourselves, to dumb down our understanding of who we are.

The problems Facebook has encountered, especially over the past two or three years, have been immense and difficult to anticipate – especially for someone with a limited understanding of human nature. Remember: Facebook's users constitute one-third of all the people on the planet. Its algorithms create loops which encourage information bubbles.

These in turn exacerbate social divisions. Not just in your community, or your city, but on a global scale. Forms of mass persuasion can be effected through disinformation with terrifying ease, and frightening results: stolen elections; incitements to violence; erosion of norms; instability.

On a more granular level, depression and malaise are caused by addiction to daily interactions with a platform that promises the world but is more often radically limiting. Facebook's ever-shifting content policies seek to control offensive material, from nudity to harmful conspiracy theories. But they cannot be implemented without recourse to long lists of exceptions and constant tweaking of the algorithms. Zuckerberg, according to Osnos, hopes "to erect a scalable system, an orderly decision tree that accounts for every eventuality and exception." He thinks that "the reason that we built this successful thing is because we just solve problem after problem after problem" – as if Facebook and the problem of its predicament in the world were itself an algorithm, an "orderly decision tree."

But perhaps it is not. Perhaps there is something wrong with the premise.

The premise, the thing that underlies all of it, is the truism that information systems need information in order to run. In our current economy, they don't just need information – they are desperate for it. The more, the better. Over the past few years we have witnessed nothing less than a worldwide data gold rush. But in companies' haste to harvest that information, the data itself tends to be trimmed of what appears extraneous or is deemed unnecessary. Why? Either because it might get in the way of fast processing and the end goal of commercial usefulness, or because it is in fact unknowable, and does not quite qualify as data because it is inherently ambiguous, unclear or unverifiable. In other words, because it is a little too much like reality. Trimming away what seems unnecessary means losing that gritty precipitate, that stubborn quotient of complicating context and sticky exception that makes reality *real*. We need to try to get our heads around this, and from there to be guided towards a crucial recognition: information and the systems that corral it (the algorithms and interfaces) *underrepresent reality.*

How could I prove this? Where is reality? What is your reality? What is mine?

I come back to Chekhov here, if only because on these questions – what is your reality? what is mine? – he is the literary equivalent of Bach: no one said it more purely, more cleanly, with so many exquisite, humanly feeling variations.

Well, and "so she married me," says Konstantin, a character in Chekhov's "The Steppe." "She's gone now to her mother's, the magpie, and while she's away I wander the steppe. I can't stay at home, it's more than I can do!"

After blurting this out, Konstantin falls silent, as people often do after blurting out what is in their hearts. In fact, this is one of the great themes in Chekhov: the idea that the very things that move us the most are the hardest to share. "The Kiss," for instance, is built around an exceptional incident in the life of Ryabovitch, "a little officer in spectacles, with sloping shoulders, and whiskers like a lynx's," which seem to say "'I am the shyest, most modest, and most undistinguished officer in the whole brigade.'" At a party thrown by a local landowner for his fellow officers, Ryabovitch meets with "a little adventure": he gets briefly lost in the big house, finds himself accidentally in a dark room, then opens a door onto a still darker room. He smells lilac and roses, hears the rustle of a dress, and a woman says, "At last!" Two arms clasp him around the neck, a cheek is pressed to his, and he receives the very kiss that gives the story its title.

It is, alas, a case of mistaken identity. The perfumed woman did not mean to kiss Ryabovitch. In the dark, she made a false assumption. She was processing incomplete data, you could say.

Ryabovitch doesn't mind. In fact, he is happy: nothing remotely like this has ever happened to him. His neck, around which soft, fragrant arms had so lately been clasped, seems to him to be "anointed with oil." He is "full of a strange new feeling which grew stronger and stronger … He wanted to dance, to talk, to run in the garden, to laugh aloud … He quite forgot that he was round-shouldered and uninteresting."

The party ends, he leaves the house, still euphoric. He and his fellow officers see a light on the other side of the river, and try to decide whether it is a camp fire or a light in a window or something else … Ryabovitch fancies that this light looks at him and winks, "as though it knew about the kiss." (I think this light is somehow a metaphor for inner life, but never mind about that: it could just be a winking light.) Ryabovitch's imagination continues to run wild. For days, he can think about nothing else. His world is changed.

Ordinary life resumes, his brigade moves on. Still, he needs to tell someone about what happened, because it has completely changed the texture and feel, the reality, the determining algorithm, of his life. Over supper, in the officers' tent, he gets a little drunk and finally pipes up: "A strange thing happened to me at those Von Rabbeks' … "

He proceeds to describe the incident in great detail. When he is done, he lapses into silence. The story has loomed so large inside him, his self is so swollen with it; but now, having spoken, "it surprised him dreadfully to find how short a time it took him to tell it. He had imagined that he could have been telling the story of the kiss till next morning."

*

Our inner lives are like this. They are swollen with tangled knots of narrative, with feelings and hurts and elaborate, fantastical dreams, which can be as enduring as mountains or as fleeting as clouds. So it is hard to look at our Facebook feeds and match what they show us with everything we feel ourselves to be. Yet stare long enough at something that claims to represent you and it can gradually come to stand in for that more inchoate, cumbersome reality.

When Ryabovitch is finished with his mystifying, frustratingly unresolved story, his companions look at him sceptically, make banal remarks and use it as a pretext to tell their own anecdotes. This is what happens, right? But Ryabovitch is nonetheless dismayed. He winces and vows "never to confide again."

On social media we are always confiding too much, always oversharing. It becomes habitual. Our child looks impressive and adorable in that school photo. We post it with a comment – hopefully nothing too embarrassing. We were at a gig last night and want to register the fact, so we post the ten seconds of footage we took. The mother of someone we know has died and we want to express sympathy – but to whom? The actual person, or their persona online, which seems so curiously incommensurate with the person we saw last Saturday?

Chekhov knew the dangers of sharing well in advance. Connecting with others can feel vital to our sanity; but every "share," as Ryabovitch discovered, can also be a betrayal of the primary, inward experience.

*

Could this be why we have art? Art is often talked about as a form of human communication, a conversation – and so it is. But on another level, the greatest art is often more like a soliloquy, an attempt to express what is inexpressible, what can never fully be shared.

Let me return, with this in mind, to Konstantin in Chekhov's other story, "The Steppe." He has just told his companions around the camp fire that he is married and in love and that being away from his new wife is driving him crazy. Konstantin "awkwardly released his feet, on which he was sitting," Chekhov tells us,

> stretched himself on the earth, and propped his head in his fists, then got up and sat down again. Everyone by now thoroughly understood that he was in love and happy, poignantly happy; his smile, his eyes, and every movement expressed fervent happiness. He could not find a place for himself, and did not know what attitude to take to keep himself from being overwhelmed by the multitude of his delightful thoughts. Having poured out his soul before these strangers, he settled down quietly at last, and, looking at the fire, sank into thought.

What happens next is a classic, soft-pedalled, perfectly Chekhovian twist. Or just a turn, really – a small change in the stream's direction, one that conveys so much about what can happen when one person's reality rubs up against another's: "At the sight of this happy man," we are told,

> everyone felt depressed and longed to be happy, too. Everyone was dreamy. Dymov got up, walked about softly by the fire, and from his walk, from the movement of his shoulder-blades, it could be seen that he was weighed down by depression and yearning. He stood still for a moment, looked at Konstantin and sat down.
>
> The camp fire had died down by now; there was no flicker, and the patch of red had grown small and dim.

I love this passage. I loved it before I had thought about it in the terms in which I am now trying to put it. So I fear I will falsify the feeling I get from it by saying anything. It has its own irreducible, nineteenth-century, Russian reality, its own obdurate resistance to being incorporated into some twenty-first-century essayist's anguished amateur philosophising. And how gauche, what a betrayal it would be to reduce this intimate campfire scene on the Russian steppe to a prescient commentary on the effects of constant exposure to the happiness of others as advertised in their Facebook feeds. I won't go there. But I will say two things that strike me about it now.

First, the unresolved movement from agitation to quietude and back again. All that standing up and sitting down, hearts full to overflowing … this, too, is what inner life is like! It is not some placid lake in a forest. It is tumultuous, provisional, unsettling.

And second, Chekhov's suggestion that happiness in one soul should be so fraught, so brimming-over, so impossible to contain, and yet so incredibly difficult to share.

One person's inner reality pressing up against another's: it's just *so very difficult*. No wonder marriage is so hard! You could even say that in most cases happiness might only be possible to share negatively. Here, at any rate, Konstantin's flooding happiness, deprived of its object ("she's gone to her mother's, the magpie"), forms the precise outline of Dymov's melancholy, so that one is left to think (as Ryabovitch thinks after sharing his adventure in "The Kiss") that it might have been better all around if Konstantin had kept his mouth shut.

Chekhov is too sensitive to say. But this is precisely the conclusion Herzog comes to in Saul Bellow's eponymous 1964 comic novel. Midway through it, Herzog is left waiting for his lover, Ramona, in a darkened room as she goes to the bathroom. Full of desire – as Konstantin is full of love – he waits and he waits, in a state beyond agitation, understanding obscurely that Ramona is trying to teach him a lesson.

"But how was he to describe this lesson? The description," writes Bellow, channelling the thought processes of Herzog, "might begin with his wild internal disorder, or even with the fact that he was quivering. And why? Because he let the entire world press in on him."

This is what it is like, Bellow is saying, to be a self. The entire world presses in on you. It comes from all corners. The pressure it exerts is what constitutes you, as a self, separate from others. Without that pressure, you are no self at all: you would dissolve and dissipate, or flap wildly, like a sail released to the wind. But what is the nature of this pressure? Help us to understand it! As Herzog waits, quivering, for Ramona to return, he lays it out for us:

> Well, for instance, what it means to be a man [he is speaking about himself]. In a city. In a century. In transition. In a mass. Transformed by science. Under organized power. Subject to tremendous controls. In a condition caused by mechanization. After the late failure of radical hopes. In a society that was no community and devalued the person. Owing to the multiplied power of numbers which made the self negligible. Which spent military billions against foreign enemies but would not pay for order at home. Which permitted savagery and barbarism in its own great cities. At the same time, the pressure of human millions who have discovered what concerted

> thoughts and efforts can do. As megatons of water shape organisms on the ocean floor. As tides polish stones.

The self, Bellow implies, is like these organisms, those stones. It is formed by pressure. But the pressure is not all angst and despair. Its flip-side is rapture, the simple euphoria of being alive, of anticipating, of desiring. To convey this, Bellow, in another passage, again invokes water (and waiting), and comes to the conclusion – like Konstantin, like Ryabovitch – that the self's euphoria, its highest bliss, is incommunicable. On this occasion, instead of waiting for his lover, Herzog is waiting for a ferry:

> he looked through the green darkness at the net of bright reflections on the bottom. He loved to think about the power of the sun, about light, about the ocean. The purity of the air moved him. There was no stain in the water, where schools of minnows swam. Herzog sighed and said to himself, "Praise God – praise God." His breathing had become freer. His heart was greatly stirred by the open horizon; the deep colors; the faint iodine pungency of the Atlantic rising from weeds and mollusks; the white, fine, heavy sand; but principally by the green transparency as he looked down to the stony bottom webbed with golden lines. Never still. If his soul could cast a reflection so brilliant, and so intensely sweet, he might beg God to make such use of him. But that would be too simple. But that would be too childish. The actual sphere is not clear like this, but turbulent, angry. A vast human action is going on. Death watches. So if you have some happiness, conceal it. And when your heart is full, keep your mouth shut also.

*

"A vast human action is going on." So it is. "Death watches." So it does! "And when your heart is full, keep your mouth shut also." Received and understood.

Private life and inner life are not the same thing. Privacy, which is linked to political freedom, refers to what you do and think away from the interested, potentially controlling eyes of others. The word itself implies the presence of power. Inner life is different. Next to it – and despite all we hear about privacy – privacy is a shallow concept.

Inner life may be elusive and impossible to define. But it can be suggested. And in important ways, it has the potential to be more substantive, and in a way more *real*, than even freedom or privacy. If we listen to people who have lost their freedom but who somehow, despite forced confinement, constant surveillance and even torture, managed to preserve their inner life, they confirm this. Yevgenia Ginzburg, who spent many years in Soviet prisons and labour camps, wrote, in *Journey into the Whirlwind*:

> I felt instinctively that even if my legs faltered and my back bent under the load of burning stones, so long as I was still capable of being moved by the sea breeze, by the brilliance of the stars and by poetry, I should continue to be a living being. I believed that if one could preserve these things in one's mind one should be able to withstand the onslaught of this world of horror.

But poetry and art don't need to come into it. Everyone has an inner life. Your inner life is not more admirable if you look at art or read novels. Not at all. But music, art and books do provide us with an opportunity to become more aware of our inner life: more attentive to it, more thoughtful about it, and perhaps more beguiled by and in awe of it.

My own sense of who I am and my place in the world comes from many things: family and friends; the people I like and don't so much like spending time with; the work I do; the home in which I live; the books I read; the pictures I look at; the music I listen to; the time I spend alone, helping others, being selfish, being active, being lazy and so on. There are times when I wonder how it all coheres. It is vexing, this business of being a self.

Quite a few years ago, reviewing Iris Murdoch's baggy book on metaphysics and morality, Galen Strawson summarised Murdoch's view of what it is to be human thus:

> We are, [Murdoch] observes, limited, imperfect, unfinished, and full of blankness and jumble. We [are] unable to domesticate the senseless rubble aspect of human life, the "ultimately unintelligible mess." We are divided creatures, distracted creatures, extended, layered, pulled apart, our minds are like ragbags, as we struggle with fear and muddle (nothing is more evident in human life), with the invincible variety, the unmasterable contingency of the world, with moments of senseless horror and "scarcely communicable frightfulness" ... Egoistic anxiety veils the world. It sets up a haze of self-protective illusion. The mind is "besieged or crowded" by selfish dream life. It is hard to exaggerate our capacity for egoistic fabrication and "rat-like fantasies." We cannot see things as they are.

An almost unsurpassable summary. So yes, being a self is difficult. Sometimes one would rather be anything else.

Is this why we run away from the idea of an inner life? Is this why we seem not to mind seeing its prestige gradually eroding? Does it explain our willingness to betray our own reality, to let external forces hollow us out and drive us towards superficiality? Does it explain our eagerness to adopt other guises, to favour performance and superficiality over introspection and honest feeling?

Heavy, earnest-sounding questions. I suspect the answers are far from straightforward.

Roland Barthes, in *A Lover's Discourse: Fragments*, spoke of how madness is usually described as an experience of depersonalisation – of being removed from oneself, as in Rimbaud's "*Je est un autre*" ("I is another"). But for Barthes, it was the other way around: being a subject, a self, an organ of pure subjectivity, was the maddening experience. "*I am not someone else*: that is what I realize with horror," he wrote. One can imagine what he meant simply by acknowledging how easy it is for humans to succumb to the feeling of being trapped inside themselves – bored by the tedium and repetition of constituting a self; envying others and their different ways of being; hamstrung by the limiting assumptions others have made about them. The modern creeds of identity politics, genetic determination and psychiatric pathology are all, to some extent, reprises of the old Calvinist doctrine of predestination (with only the conclusion, that you are either eternally damned or saved, diluted): *You are you*, they insist. *You are not anything else. We will know you and treat you as such.*

It is a heavy burden to carry. And perhaps it asks too much of people to expect them to be coherent. Being assigned a self can be like being diagnosed with a condition. This partially explains, I think, the appeal of online avatars, gaming and the whole business of gleefully hatching alternative identities. It's the virtual equivalent of putting on masks and going to orgies. The permission it gives … the potential it creates … the longed-for escape from the madness of being singular … the repertoire of possibilities seems so vast, so liberating …

And yet isn't this, too, a kind of madness? If being a self is hard, at times even maddeningly hard, being "someone else" is not necessarily a path to sanity. But perhaps sanity is not the goal?

We are in an angry moment. It is incredible, on Facebook and Twitter and in comment threads, to see how quickly people fall into abuse, sarcasm and general nastiness. The parts of people's psyches that were to some extent suppressed are now spilling out in all directions. The terrible strain of pretending that other person over there is just as important as I am, that we are equal, or that the other side may have a point is proving too much to bear.

Decorum is out the window. Online, a new dispensation rules. There is no deep shame in behaving badly. ("Wherefore," asks Edmund in *King Lear*, "should I stand in the plague of custom? ... Why brand they us with base? with baseness? bastardy? base, base? ... Now, gods, stand up for bastards!") Taunting is in. A female student in a hijab is surrounded and heckled by fellow students, who call her a terrorist. Black students get on a bus only to be told by other students to sit in the back. Female current affairs hosts with decades of experience are barked at and sexually humiliated for daring to speak. Swastikas appear in the boys' bathroom at a school with high numbers of Jewish students.

It's interesting. The artists who feel most in tune with what is going on right now are not, by and large, overtly political. Political ways of framing reality, and political speech, have less and less traction these days. Hence the appeal of mavericks and "straight-shooting," I-tell-it-like-I see-it candidates. The carefully crafted speech of more conventional candidates – those who heed the demographic analyses and focus-group research and who hope to maximise their appeal by alienating the fewest voters possible – has a strange way of not really applying to anyone. (That, in a nutshell, was Hillary Clinton's problem.) The same, unfortunately, is true of most well-intentioned political art. The artists who speak most cogently to the present are interested in conveying what the painter Francis Bacon called "the brutality of fact." This can be salutary in an age of fake news.

Bacon is himself exemplary. His portraits come out of a dark European tradition that includes Hieronymous Bosch, James Ensor, Pablo Picasso and Max Beckmann. They dramatise a tension between the psyche's darker compulsions and a pressure felt within civilised society to conform, to stifle emotions, not to lash out. Bacon invented a new visual language for this tension. He drew on those forerunners in art, but also on photographs in medical textbooks, the films of Luis Buñuel and Sergei Eisenstein, the stop-motion photographs of Eadweard Muybridge, and news images of twentieth-century violence. Think, for instance, of the pinched and slightly blurred look in Donald Trump's eyes when he is not getting his way, feels hard done by or cannot say what he really feels. His micro-expressions – the fleeting twitches, the flashes of furious indignation – hint at a mind incapable of composure. They find gorgeous equivalents in the smeared, distended expressions of Bacon's portraits, which capture the human psyche at the very moment when composure breaks down and the animal – adrenalised, alert, ready to snarl – is revealed.

Both Bacon and Bosch have been huge influences on Gareth Sansom, an Australian artist I consider to be one of the most compelling at work anywhere in the world. His hectic, splintered paintings – partly figurative, partly abstract – over the past two decades have come to feel like enactments, in paint, of the mind's dividedness, its frantic scrabbling and ceaseless unspooling; its loose threads and tangled knots; and of the pressure it is always under – unstinting pressure.

Society, like the self, is divided. People are on a short fuse. They are looking for – and finding – like-mindedness. In some cases, for the reassurance of platitudes. In others, for permission to make those ugly faces, to express the contempt that burns beneath the scuffed veneer of civility. In crowds, at protests, at rallies and especially online, they feel an expanded licence to say and do things they wouldn't dare elsewhere. Sometimes they hide behind a political placard. Given the right setting, they might even throw up a Nazi salute.

Plenty of artists have been interested in this side of our psyches. Gillian Wearing, from Britain, once made a series of photographs called "Signs That Say What You Want Them to Say and Not Signs That Say What Someone Else Wants You to Say." Members of the public were asked to pose for the camera while holding up signs on which they had written whatever they chose in the moment. Some were pitiful and funny – gorgeously English, like a song by The Smiths: "The last holiday abroad was nice but I can't afford it." Or: "Southwark Council hopeless." Others were just hilariously inappropriate. But the most famous showed a young, white, well-groomed man in a business suit holding up a sign on which he had written, "I'M DESPERATE."

In another work, called "Confess All On Video. Don't Worry, You Will Be in Disguise. Intrigued? Call Gillian … ," Wearing showed ten people in succession wearing repellent masks: ugly wigs, a penis nose, and so on. Liberated by an anonymity that was tilted deliberately towards hostility, the participants who answered the ad found a bizarre new confidence in self-exposure. Sounding like a pervert, it seemed, could be something to be proud of if you weren't going to have to face up to the audience you were addressing. Wearing's interest in doubleness, and in the permission we grant ourselves to express primitive feelings, seems apt at a time when social media and online comment threads have unleashed astonishing toxicity.

*

A few times, when I have taken my two kids to the Museum of Fine Arts in Boston, where we live, I have invited them to pose on either side of a sculpture by Franz Xaver Messerschmidt and to make an ugly face for the camera. Each time, they've accepted. It is fun to make faces. Near the end of his life, Messerschmidt, who was Austrian, turned out a series of sixty-nine sculptures in alabaster and lead known as "*Charakterköpfe*," or "Character Heads." He would tense his body, contort his face and record what he saw in the mirror in three dimensions with extraordinary fidelity and precision. Ostensibly, these studies, of which forty-nine survive, were Messerschmidt's contribution to the pseudoscience of physiognomy – the notion that facial expression can be studied as an accurate index to character (which of course is nonsense). Accordingly, the sculptures were given titles such as "A Hypocrite and Slanderer," "The Ill-Humored Man" and, in this case, "The Hypochondriac."

But I believe these titles lead us astray. I believe the sculptures are really about the deeper human urge to pull faces. Messerschmidt embarked on his "Character Heads" back in his native Bavaria, after his glittering career, replete with royal commissions, had been derailed. He was forced to resign from the Vienna Academy in 1774, just five years after he had been made professor. He seemed to be struggling with private demons. Mental illness has been assumed. So the "Character Heads" can be seen as part of Messerschmidt's attempt to exorcise his demons. But they might also make us wonder where this strange compulsion to pull faces comes from.

There is a great passage about face-pulling in Alice Munro's "The Beggar Maid." A woman has seen, across an airport terminal, late at night, her ex-lover. She feels a nostalgic tug, an urge to go up and touch him, to "surprise him with his happiness." But before she can, he turns around. He sees her. His reaction is spontaneous: "He made a face at her. It was a truly hateful, savagely warning, face; infantile, self-indulgent, yet calculated; it was a timed explosion of disgust and loathing. It was hard to believe. But she saw it."

"She," in Munro's story, is a television reporter. In her work, she has sometimes sensed in otherwise composed and dignified subjects speaking live on air a similar desire to make a face. These people – "skillful politicians and witty liberal bishops and honored humanitarians" and so on – "were longing to sabotage themselves, to make a face or say a dirty word."

"Was this," wonders Munro's female protagonist, "the face they all wanted to make? To show somebody, to show everybody? They wouldn't do it, though; they wouldn't get the chance. Special circumstances were required. A lurid unreal place, the middle of the night, a staggering unhinging weariness, the sudden, hallucinatory appearance of your true enemy."

The internet has made this "lurid unreal place" available to us twenty-four hours a day.

*

Your true enemy. One begins to wonder where such a person might be found. How close to home? How intimate? What if, upon attending closely to our inner lives, we were to find something other than what we were looking for? (When Edgar Degas said that "the people you love the most are the people you could hate the most," there was always the possibility that he might be talking about himself.)

The reality is that it is not easy operating in different registers, on different frequencies, with a secret inner life and another self for public consumption. The work of cohering as a self is hard, and ongoing. It is therefore tempting to think that it would be easier if we dispensed with the aspects of ourselves that have depth, that are carved out of the difficult process of self-knowledge. It may feel easier to exist on the surface. That way, we could protect ourselves from what happens when external events become inward occasions. Because external events do. They are always impinging on inner life, and the work of making it all cohere is never done.

Attending to our true selves may reveal things we don't want or can't bear to see. When others give up on the attempt to cultivate their deeper, better selves, it can be similarly confounding. It can feel as if they have given way, like a dam wall under overwhelming pressure. In Philip Roth's *American Pastoral*, the ostensibly virtuous, impressively coherent main character, Swede Levov, finds himself reflecting on this:

> That people were manifold creatures didn't come as a surprise to the Swede, even if it was a bit of a shock to realize it anew when someone let you down. What was astonishing to him was how people seemed to run out of their own being, run out of whatever the stuff was that made them who they were and, drained of themselves, turn into the sort of people they would once have felt sorry for. It was as though while their lives were rich and full they were secretly sick of themselves and couldn't wait to dispose of their sanity and their health and all sense of proportion so as to get down to that other self, the *true* self, who was a wholly deluded fuckup. It was as though being in tune with life was an accident that might sometimes befall the fortunate young but was otherwise something for which human beings lacked any real affinity.

If the true self really is a "wholly deluded fuckup" – inconstant, untrustworthy, prone to extremes of self-sabotage – where does that leave social life – the business of engaging with and relating to other people? Where, indeed, does it leave love life? How are we to connect with others?

NIGHTHAWKS

A few pages into Rachel Cusk's novel *Outline*, the narrator, a writer flying to Athens from London, is talking with the Greek man seated beside her. He has with him a popular novel by Wilbur Smith. But because he has picked the narrator for a writer with a more highbrow sensibility, he is embarrassed to be caught with such a trashy-looking novel (no offence to Wilbur Smith: I read everything he wrote when I was a teenager). So he mumbles something awkward and stashes it away in his bag.

The narrator observes this. But, "as it happened," she tells us, "I was no longer interested in literature as a form of snobbery or even of self-definition – I had no desire to prove that one book was better than another: in fact," she says – and this, for me, was the key part – "if I read something I admired I found myself increasingly disinclined to mention it at all. What I knew personally to be true had come to seem unrelated to the process of persuading others. I did not, any longer, want to persuade anyone of anything."

We know by this point that the narrator is living in the aftermath of a marital break-up. So it's unclear – and we remain in the dark about this throughout the novel – whether the condition she describes is related to her own slightly unanchored, shell-shocked state of mind, or whether it reflects some deeper recognition about art: a recognition that, if you think about it, would militate not only against friendly recommendations, but against art criticism, and education, and the whole edifice of assumptions on which our marvellous museums and what we call "culture" as a whole are constructed. Because of course, if what you know personally to be true no longer feels related to the process of persuading others, all those things could be said to be in serious trouble.

Either way, the passage in *Outline* articulated – with uncanny accuracy – how I myself had begun to feel about a year ago, before I returned to Sydney with my family for a twelve-month sabbatical. For a while there, I no longer wanted to persuade anyone of anything. If I saw a great painting, or read a wonderful book, I had little or no urge to share the news. The idea of explaining why I thought a work of art was great, or of persuading others to see the quality I saw in it, had begun to seem almost pointless, and somehow foolish. This condition may or may not have been a malaise to take seriously. But it could be said to be a problem if you are an art critic – if your job is precisely to present opinions on art and exhibitions every week in a public forum, and then to tweet about those opinions, to put them on Instagram and Facebook, and from there to count up clicks and comments and engagement time, presumably with a view to measuring your own worth, your opinions' persuasiveness and your ultimate value to some unspoken larger social enterprise.

Interestingly, Cusk's confession – that if she read something she admired she found herself increasingly disinclined to mention it at all – chimed with something the painter Lucian Freud once said, an offhand-sounding statement which for some reason I have always loved. "When you find something very moving," he said, "it almost makes you want to know less about it – rather like when falling in love, you don't want to meet the parents."

It struck me that if the narrator's opinion in Cusk's novel was an expression of alienation or disaffection, Lucian Freud's formulation seemed to put a more positive – not to say humorous – spin on the same impulse. Not wanting to know more about something – not wanting to share it or analyse it or in any way speak about it, for fear of spoiling it – was something that happened, Freud implied, when you were deeply moved by it – when you were in some way falling in love.

It seems, as I noted, like a casual thing to have said. A bit of intellectual loose change. But over the years, as it has rattled around in my head, I have to say this idea has become more and more magnetic for me, and almost darkly seductive. In my mind, it connects art not only with falling in love, but with inner life, and perhaps even with belief itself.

I don't necessarily mean religious belief. I simply mean the kind of belief that makes it possible to locate our true selves, to cohere, and to proceed from there with a feeling of agency in the mystery, the specific quiddity, of our own lives. The kind of belief that makes it possible not to get stuck in endless knowingness. (Keats, in his letters, lamented the plight of "a man who cannot feel that he has a personal identity unless he has made up his mind about everything.") "Knowingness" I define as a condition of mind that, affecting shrewdness or wisdom, is actually the product of received or predigested ideas of how to be. You see it every day. It is all over the internet. It is at odds, I have come to think, with inner life.

*

Chekhov, in "The Steppe," describes a character called Vassya:

> He was so long-sighted that the brown steppe for him was always full of interest. He had only to look into the distance to see a fox, a hare, a bustard, or some other animal keeping at a distance from men. There was nothing strange in seeing a hare running away or a flying bustard – everyone crossing the steppes could see them; but it was not vouchsafed to everyone to see wild animals in their own haunts when they were not running or hiding, nor looking about them in alarm. Yet Vassya saw foxes playing, hares washing themselves with their paws, bustards preening their wings and hammering out their hollow nests. Thanks to this keenness of sight, Vassya had, besides the world seen by everyone, another world of his own, accessible to no one else, and probably a very beautiful one, for when he saw something and was in raptures over it, it was impossible not to envy him.

What is it about Vassya that is impossible not to envy? His special ability to see, and the magical sights this ability bestows on him? Certainly. But sight is just sight. Chekhov is driving at something deeper, and to convey this he offers another of his little Chekhovian twists or inversions. From the external world, he switches surreptitiously to an internal vista – to inner life. "Thanks to this keenness of sight, Vassya had, besides the world seen by everyone, another world of his own, accessible to no one else, and probably a very beautiful one."

It's embarrassing to admit, but I read this passage aloud at my wedding when, after all the speeches (among them a devastating and hilarious indictment of my character by my best man), it was finally my turn to get up and say something. My wife, I thought, had – and still has – something of Vassya in her: an enviable ability to see things (in her case, in people) that others cannot. The things she sees are not actionable, as such – they have no particular use value; you could not feed them into an algorithm and get the result you were looking for. But I see her accessing these worlds when she has left the door to the music room in our house ajar, and I glimpse her with her students. I see it, too, when she is with our kids, or her friends, who love her, as I do, because there are things they can say with her that they don't seem to be able to say in quite the same way with anyone else.

These things she perceives are like portals to the inner lives of others: her friends, her children, her students and the rest of us who share her world. It is subtle, this ability, and I may, if I am annoyed with her (how hard marriage is!), go weeks or months without really registering it. But there is a passage in Don DeLillo's *White Noise* – a banal domestic scene the narrator, a professor of Hitler Studies, observes with his tender, ironic eye – that gets close to what I am talking about:

> I watched Denise make a mental comparison between her mother's running clothes and the wet bag she'd dumped in the compactor. I could see it in her eyes, a sardonic connection. It was these secondary levels of life, these extrasensory flashes and floating nuances of being, these pockets of rapport forming unexpectedly, that made me believe we were a magic act, adults and children together, sharing unaccountable things.

When you read this passage, you may wonder how a comparison between running clothes and a wet bag in a compactor could possibly give rise to such "extrasensory flashes and floating nuances of being." And yet this is what domestic life is like, isn't it? Inner lives rubbing up against one another, for better or for worse. It happens also while talking in bed, late at night, where intimate things are disclosed, in what DeLillo calls "a form of self-renewal and a gesture of custodial trust." During these intimate, late-night disclosures, no detail, writes DeLillo,

> must be left out, not even a dog with ticks or a neighbor's boy who ate an insect on a dare. The smell of pantries, the sense of empty afternoons, the feel of things as they rained across our skin, things as facts and passions, the feel of pain, loss, disappointment, breathless delight. In these night recitations we create a space between things as we felt them at the time and as we speak them now. This is the space reserved for irony, sympathy and fond amusement, the means by which we rescue ourselves from the past.

DeLillo here is describing intimacy, yes – but also inner life ("the feel of things as they rained across our skin, things as facts and passions, the feel of pain, loss, disappointment, breathless delight"). Inner life, it turns out, need not always be the part of us that is hidden. It *can* be communicated. Admittedly, special circumstances are required. A quiet, unreal place, the middle of the night, weariness, the sudden, hallucinatory appearance of your true love.

*

In the right circumstances – and they are rare – inner life is drawn out of us, bridging the chasms that separate not only the distinct parts of ourselves but also ourselves from others. There are paintings which depict this, paintings of one inner life reaching out to connect with another. One of my favorites is Chardin's "Young Schoolmistress." It hangs in the

National Gallery in London; another version, titled "The Little Schoolmistress," is in the National Gallery in Washington, DC. A young person – she looks scarcely more than a girl herself – is shown instructing a smaller, round-faced child. She directs the child's attention to what is written on papers set out on a wooden cabinet. The child looks down attentively, trying – perhaps failing – to understand. Leaning forward, the young teacher looks to the child, awaiting the flicker of comprehension her instruction, her patience, deserve.

It is as simple as that. Why is it so moving?

There is a tenderness, I suppose, in the way the young teacher's body is inclined towards her charge, and a lovely, telling tension between the formality of the situation and both subjects' youth. The painting was exhibited at the Salon of 1740, and engraved that same year by François-Bernard Lépicié. A chauvinistic inscription was added to the engraving: "If this charming child takes on so well the serious air and imposing manner of a schoolmistress, may one not think pretence and artfulness come to the fair sex no later than birth?"

But the inscription, of course, has it entirely wrong. The painting's tenderness has nothing to do with pretence or artfulness. Chardin has instead depicted a moment so intimate, so absorbed and absorbent, that there is something hallowed about it. You can feel a nimbus of attention as much around the painting itself as around the focused scene Chardin depicts. The way he has captured the girl's profile; the way her upper lip protrudes slightly; the pursed but in no way pinched or disapproving set of her lips; the unusually thin slits of her patient, focused eyes; the very slight tilt of her head; the blush on both their cheeks, and the harmonious colouring throughout. (I love especially the powdery blue, tinged with green, of the teacher's dress sleeve against the brown, shadowed background.) To the young, round-faced child, so small in the face of all that is knowable, the older girl must seem a kind of angel.

What passes between teachers and students? What occurs when one person takes on the formal but intimate role of instructing another? As the son of two teachers, the husband of another, and the father of two students, I often wonder. The relationship is never the same. It is often unpleasant, or in some way dysfunctional. (When Günther Grass, in *The Tin Drum*, wrote of catching "a whiff of that school smell ... which is more intimate than any perfume in the world," he was describing a complex perfume, evoking both the beautiful aroma of childhood susceptibility and the bad odour of school dysfunction.) But when the teacher–student relationship is working, something enigmatic is allowed to occur. One party assumes a level of care that is serious but not neurotically so (it falls short, that's to say, of the duty of parenthood). The other is there rarely by choice but with the understanding that she might learn something. There are many ways in which the arrangement can misfire, most of them having to do with the absence of choice on the part of the student. But there is both suppleness and an intimacy to it that allows for the forms of absorption, the floating pockets of rapport, that Chardin so beautifully captured.

One of the things the teacher–student relationship does is establish a formal structure for the hope, the intuition, that you are not alone. You are not alone with your inexperience and ignorance. And perhaps just as importantly, you are not alone with your inner life. It is an inherently contradictory dynamic. We need to know we are not alone, and yet we hanker for opportunities to be left alone – to woo those distant parts of ourselves; to put aside the chores and distractions; to liberate ourselves from the idea that our days should be carved up into discrete parcels of attention to be fought over by companies whose whole raison d'être is to find ways to monetise those parcels.

The space and the time to be with oneself is something school used to deliver – sometimes just in the quiet periods of class when we were expected to get on with work but would instead find ourselves, in the first days of autumn, staring out the window; sometimes in more unexpected circumstances. Remembering his school years in *Boyhood*, his third-person memoir, J. M. Coetzee wrote:

> Mr. Gouws uses the cane as much as any other teacher. But his favourite punishment, when the class has been too noisy for too long, is to order them to put down their pens, shut their books, clasp their hands behind their heads, close their eyes, and sit absolutely still. Save for Mr. Gouws's footfalls as he patrols up and down the rows, there is absolute silence in the room. From the eucalyptus trees around the quadrangle comes the tranquil cooing of doves. This is a punishment he could endure forever, with equanimity: the doves, the soft breathing of the boys around him.

As much as the soft, proximate breathing of those boys, the doves cooing in the eucalypts feel to me like stand-ins for inner life. The two things – the inside breathing, the outside cooing – are clearly separate and yet, at some deeper level, they are indivisible. Inside and outside; the knowable and unknowable; the communicable and the incommunicable; his life; the boys' lives; the birds' – all are folded together like some intricate piece of inverted origami. (There is a related image in Annie Proulx's *The Shipping News*, in which the main character hears a bird hammering at the window and wants to shoo it away before it wakes his aunt and the two young girls: "It seemed the bird was trying to break from the closed room of sea and rock and sky into the vastness of his bare chamber.") These images are poetic. They are not rational. But they are, in their different ways, circling around a phenomenon they can only approach obliquely – this thing I have called inner life. And they are all concerned, it seems to me, with "connecting solitudes."

*

The term is the art critic Peter Schjeldahl's. He was writing about Edward Hopper's "Nighthawks." One of the most famous pictures of the twentieth century, "Nighthawks" shows three customers and an employee in a glass-fronted diner on a bleak, deserted street corner. For many, the painting evokes loneliness. It carries, too, a sort of existentialist glamour, later enhanced by Hollywood (a famous pastiche of the painting by

Gottfried Helnwein called "Boulevard of Broken Dreams" replaces the anonymous figures with Marilyn Monroe, James Dean, Humphrey Bogart and Elvis Presley).

Schjeldahl was talking about the problem of paintings which have become so popular, so well-known (think Grant Wood's "American Gothic," Edvard Munch's "The Scream," or Leonardo's "Mona Lisa") that they exist more as a shared resource in a communal image bank than as a specific image with any hope of activating an individual's imagination. How to get back to the thing itself, before it hardened into a cliché? Schjeldahl did the only thing you can do: he lasered in on the painting itself, questioning the widespread assumption that the figures in it are lonely. Hopper's diner, he wrote, evokes

> impenetrable private ordeals, and no less enigmatic compensations, to the passerby whose viewpoint each of us assumes as we gaze. The word routinely used to describe Hopper's work, "loneliness," doesn't apply to the depicted characters, who are doing fine in their iffy ways. The inexact term gestures toward a hardly communicable feeling, which we enjoy as we would a melancholy song that is beautiful and true. A similar dynamic characterises all serious painting – it's an art that is cultivated in solitude to bear fruit in the fortuitous, real space and the chosen, real time of incarnate viewers.

The key phrase here is "hardly communicable feeling," and the concomitant recognition that it need not imply loneliness. Aloneness, yes. But that is different. Unlike the artificial connectivity of social media, great art, as Schjeldahl wrote, puts "you on your own, responsive and responsible in your aloneness."

*

As software, social media platforms such as Facebook are relatively primitive. They don't approach what is made possible by the growing proximity to human consciousness that scientists are already achieving in the field of artificial intelligence. It goes without saying that Siri and her avatar friends, who are getting more sophisticated and responsive all the time, have a great deal to offer. It remains incredible to think that one can now travel in a car along complicated multi-lane freeways and tricky backstreets without having to touch the steering wheel or brake.

In the emotional and psychological realms, too, there has been, as one of Rachel Cusk's characters in her novel *Transit* points out, "a great harvest of language and information from life." It may even be, as the same character says, that "the faux-human is growing more substantial and more relational than the original" – that there is potentially more tenderness to be had from a machine than from our fellow humans. "After all," the character continues, "the mechanized interface was the distillation not of one but of many." In fact, it could even be soothing to think that this chorus of distilled wisdom, helpfulness, compassion, or love, is affixed not to any one person, but to an aggregation of people, a sort of harvest of knowingness, which seems "to come" both "from everywhere and nowhere." Since the individuals with whom we share our inner lives have such limitless power to hurt us, the erosion of individuality, notes the character, could also be seen as the erosion of the power to hurt.

It's a droll, deliberately provocative argument, which nonetheless raises real questions. What is lost in this new, algorithmic scenario, where the power to hurt has been diluted? Perhaps it is simply the grit, the texture, the adhesiveness that comes from a specific engagement with a specific experience by a specific human being. One inner life aiming to connect with another – and in this way, providing an alternative to the manufactured, mathematical consensus. Such attempted connections remain more meaningful, in human terms, than relying on a disembodied, soup-like aggregation. But perhaps I am wrong. What it is to be human appears to be changing quickly.

*

Today, being human means being distracted. It is our new default setting. We are almost all living in a state of constant distraction. In the meantime, our deepest feelings are being flushed out, forced to the surface, dissolved in the endless chatter of our heavily mediated environment, trampled underfoot in the rush to be heard, and seen. All of this has produced, as Edward Mendelson wrote:

> a newly pervasive, permeable, and transient sense of self, in which much of the experience, feeling, and emotion that used to exist within the confines of the self, in intimate relations, and in tangible unchanging objects ... has migrated to the phone, to the 'digital cloud,' and to the shape-shifting judgments of the crowd.

In this new dispensation, it can seem as if searchlights are raking back and forth across the surface of our separate selves, bleaching and blurring everything they illuminate, and turning the idea of the soul itself – which was always perhaps to some extent a fiction, but at its best a dark, extravagant, spellbinding one – into a fungible entity, a binary construct of ones and zeros. It is humiliating to think how complicit we have been in letting this rich but difficult inheritance – the mystery of being alive, of being mortal, of being alone and open to love – be traduced by such limited worldviews.

There is no simple answer to the question of who we are. And, of course, from that it follows that there is no simple answer to the question of how we should relate to one another. There is something preposterous in the very use of the word "should" in this context. "Should" according to whom? With what end in mind? You would need to be very sure of yourself to say.

What I get from Chekhov – and from Cusk and Coetzee and DeLillo and Munro, as well as from Chardin and Hopper and Bacon and all the rest – has nothing to do with a desire to return to some old idea of the self, inflected by nostalgia. What I get is an apprehension that we are alone, and an artistic response to the implications of this. Our mortality makes our aloneness inevitable. There is no getting around it. We will die, and everything that is in our heads and hearts, the whole edifice of connections between what we know and how we feel, who we love and what we have struggled with, will disappear with us. It is very hard not to panic in the face of this fact.

One response to this panic, it seems to me, is to disperse ourselves, by being as widely visible as possible. Social media, and the internet generally, make this feel possible, to an unprecedented degree. They allow us to lay before the world (in the hope that the world will be watching) the things we love, the things we hate, and a mediated image of our lives that can seem to rescue us from the threat of oblivion.

But perhaps, in laying ourselves out in this way, we are excavating too much, forcing too many fragile things into the light. We cannot go back to old ways of being in the world. Chekhov's time, his way of being, is not coming back, and nor would we want it to. But it may be that, even in this brave new interconnected world, we can find ways to pay attention again to our solitude, daring to hope that we might connect that solitude to the solitude of others.

*

Chekhov was a prolific writer. It can be strange to think that he put limits on himself, that he kept anything back. But in a letter he wrote to a friend in March 1886, he talked about the lengths he went to not to "waste" on any story "the images and scenes dear to me which – God knows why – I have kept carefully hidden." Two years later, he wrote in another letter of "the images which seem best to me, which I love and jealously guard lest I spend and spoil them."

"All that I now write," he continued, "displeases and bores me, but what sits in my head interests, excites, and moves me." Chekhov was talking, of course, of his inner life. And in these simple, unforced statements, he showed how dearly he wanted to protect it.

FOLLOW
THE
LEADER

Correspondence

Katharine Murphy

We should be looking for strong leaders to follow, not a strongman, Laura Tingle writes at the end of her essay about leadership. Given the quality of the analyst, this conclusion is, of course, very persuasive. But if we examine our addled politics, both domestically and internationally, this worthy objective seems ambitious, almost ludicrous. Imagine happening upon such a leader, a politician capable of exhibiting strength and purpose in the maelstrom of contemporary public life, a political leader to inspire hope. Even if one had the good fortune to happen upon such a person, would their colleagues permit them to lead, given the past decade of Australian politics has produced leaders with brutally short shelf lives – prime ministers programmed with planned obsolescence, as if they were iPhones?

The story behind this unmooring is multifactorial, but Kevin Rudd and Tony Abbott are catalytic figures in different ways. Rudd increased the pace of politics when he gave himself the objective of trying to set the agenda from Opposition, rather than respond to the government's agenda. The new Labor man felt he had to puncture the somnolent tempo of the Howard era as part of grabbing the nation's attention and positioning himself as putative prime minister in a matter of months.

Rudd's arrival in the Lodge coincided with the profound technological disruption that created the rolling news cycle. Australian politics became a spectator sport, with the action from Canberra delivered blow by blow. Public life began to assume the death-match atmospherics of a football final. The rise of death-match atmospherics created the perfect conditions for the rise of Tony Abbott and his cacophonous politics of destruction. Just as Rudd had changed the pace of politics from Opposition, Abbott changed the tenor of politics from Opposition, elevating wrecking to the core of the enterprise. Abbott eschewed the business of deliberation and compromise, enterprises once considered to be the heart of the democratic model, and inculcated a sense of crisis in order to question the legitimacy of his political opponents.

Australian politics is still battling these two influences – an unrelenting pace narrated too often with hyperbolic, valueless commentary; and a culture where destruction is considered a legitimate tool of war – and they are poisoning political leadership in this country.

Mostly, Australian politics has been sleepwalking into the current nadir, reluctant to face up to or articulate the truth, lest some tribal taboo be broken, but interestingly, during the last leadership challenge, when Malcolm Turnbull was driven from office by the animus-fuelled faction that couldn't abide him, something cracked inside the Liberal Party, and despair tumbled out.

The despair was heard primarily in a small chorus of women's voices, women speaking critically about party culture, a culture where unhinged things seemed to happen over and over, and dissenters to the unhinging were bullied by self-appointed powerbrokers into submission and quiescence. The Victorian Liberal Julia Banks, who announced she would leave political life after enduring the leadership fracas, felt and said implicitly that the national interest could not be served by staying, which is about as damning as self-assessments get. Despair was new, a break from previous practice. Whether despair leads to anything productive remains moot.

The whole political ecosystem is impatient. The honeymoons once enjoyed by new prime ministers are short, and highly conditional, if they materialise at all. Voters are drifting away from partisan loyalties, and this seemingly inexorable drift to political disruptors is enabled by the major parties themselves, because the major parties have forgotten the premium they once offered voters was stability. Because voters are drifting, there is a preoccupation with "the base" that has become a strange form of religion, a fundamentalism which can pit the interests of political movements against the wishes of the mainstream, thereby intensifying the estrangement.

In an age where politics and public activism structures itself around the permanent campaign – given the campaign is a mechanism always on the hunt for a crisis, given the crisis has become a focal point to recruit foot soldiers and raise money – compromise is also deeply out of fashion, which is highly problematic given progress depends on it.

In one of the most interesting political speeches of 2018, the Senate president, Scott Ryan, pointed out what should be obvious: the greatest successes of Australian politics had come from "compromise and negotiation" and the use of parliamentary process to resolve competing points of view.

In a message both to colleagues and the ecosystem as a whole, Ryan noted that "the idea that compromise is wrong, that negotiation to achieve one objective and move onto another, represents a lost political opportunity for a contest or selling out is not one that has been rewarded in Australia." Ryan observed that John Howard and the then National Party leader, Tim Fischer, "bore an enormous political cost among many of their traditional supporters when instituting national gun laws, but they weren't relentlessly attacked as abandoning the base simply by virtue of challenging supporters, even on such a difficult issue." The point being that the interest of the nation should always rank ahead of sectional interest, even if the sectional interest happens to be familial; and the art of politics is explaining the necessity of action to the losers and cushioning the impact of change – something that Australian politics once excelled at.

Tingle puts her finger squarely on the challenge by pointing out that leaders need to rebuild the national debate and protect other voices within it, a form of housekeeping that requires something more profound than dishing up perpetual motion and perpetual conflict. It requires political leaders to see themselves as part of an organism rather than as a saviour or a subduer, and to give priority to the health of the organism over their own short-term imperatives or corrosive acts of one-upmanship. It requires politicians to understand they are temporary custodians of a valuable tradition, rather than succumbing to the gravitational pull of dabbling in reactionary populism because it's easier than attempting a course correction.

This sense of politicians valuing themselves as institutional forces, a politics where ego plays second fiddle to the articulation of collective purpose and responsibility, is a very big ask, particularly at this juncture. As Tingle points out, we are now at the tail-end of the global financial crisis – the greatest economic shock since the Depression – and we are witnessing a global upheaval in politics: the rise of autocracies and strongman politics and the decline of democracy and multilateralism. The world, she notes, is becoming more irrational, and we cannot assume that what follows from that is orderly.

In short, it is hard, and getting harder, to be hopeful. Not impossible. But hard.

Katharine Murphy

FOLLOW THE LEADER

Correspondence

Scott Ryan

Some may say that, as a serving politician, I have a conflict in commenting on Laura Tingle's essay; indeed, some may argue that I am partially responsible for the situation she outlines. But that position also provides a unique perspective.

Laura outlines many challenges, some the result of changing technology, particularly media; others, of the way the world has changed in the past decade, for example with the Great Recession in North America and Europe. Australia has not been immune to these changes, as Laura outlines, even if they have not resulted in the same electoral shocks we have seen elsewhere.

At its core, politics is a means of compromising over competing objectives. This occurs through democratic determination, where one mandate or proposed program earns legitimacy through elections, and through the political and parliamentary process, where the great bulk of decisions that aren't determined electorally are managed by a government through administration and the parliament. In both democratic determination and the parliamentary process, some element of "trade-off," or compromise, is critical.

First, this occurs inside political parties, which serve as forums for compromise among people with similar values and priorities. Second, it occurs through parliament, where executives are held accountable, and legislation and budgets are proposed and approved. Without these mechanisms, politics becomes less a forum for managing competing priorities and more one for conflict over them. There have always been – indeed, should be – elements of compromise and conflict, but recent trends and examples indicate that the balance has tipped in favour of the latter.

Why is this? A distinction must be made between those issues that are more open to compromise and those that are not. The rise of social issues that previously didn't form a substantial part of the domestic political debate reflects this. There is no compromise available on an issue such as same-sex marriage: it is either legislated or it is not. One can more easily compromise on economic issues, through either a less radical program (be it interventionist or deregulatory) or by managing the costs of change through adjustment and support packages. Australia has long been successful at the latter, but our political system is finding it more difficult to deal with social issues that require a binary yes/no answer.

Debates around such yes/no issues serve to polarise views across the political spectrum, and to simplify the terms of political debate. They assist in forming "camps" that then help determine the future political agenda and create the groups that participate in it. The impact of the decade-long debate on same-sex marriage can be seen across the political spectrum, both in the issues that arose alongside it and subsequently, and on those who participate in such debates. I am not judging this, just observing it.

Social issues are also, by their nature, more suited to the new media world of Twitter and other social media. Positions are taken in moral terms, and one can be for or against a moral question in 140 characters more easily than one can explain the deregulation of the dairy industry, or why tax and welfare reform is necessary. The new media world makes the explanation of compromise much more difficult, as the "trade-off" is usually complex and harder to explain. The negotiations between Peter Reith and Cheryl Kernot over workplace relations reform in 1997, or those between John Howard and Peter Costello and Meg Lees over the GST in 1999, are not well suited to short slogans that make older sound-bites sound positively thesis-like. I cannot help but think this new media world, both in production and consumption by citizens, is one reason these issues that are more suited to it have become more prominent in debate.

However, that can't be the only reason. Laura outlines a decline in the lack of trust in institutions and leaders. This is critical when considering the difficulty in compromising on complex issues. Without trust in the key players, be they politicians, business leaders or even community and church leaders, compromise becomes more difficult. The process of compromise plays a role in generating consent among citizens and groups, but if there is less trust in those "in the room" or in parliament, then a direct consequence will be a decline in support for the outcome.

Compromise can also be easily misrepresented. In my Alfred Deakin Lecture in August this year, I provided a few examples where compromise was once lauded. It was seen as a sign of maturity and a valid way to achieve one's objectives, while at the same time securing consent from many of those who might not share them. In the modern political era, though, what was once applauded as compromise is attacked as "selling out." Or, even worse, as attacking or abandoning "the base." Now, to reflect the values of one's supporters is important in politics, but occasionally real leadership requires challenging their views and persuading them of alternatives. The great example of this, of course, is John Howard and Tim Fischer on firearms, for which the overwhelming majority of the country remains grateful. The modern challenge in this area is again reflected in the 140-character terms of debate, where "attacking the base" has too often taken the place of debate rather than genuinely querying policy and seeking an explanation or persuasion.

Finally, Laura also highlights the increasing simplicity of political debate. I've outlined some trends that I think explain this, but there is another: a lack of humility. When I was a minister, many people and groups came to see me with "all you need to do is … " proposals. Sometimes they were blatantly pushing their own barrow, sometimes genuinely altruistic. I would often commence my response with: "But there are no easy solutions. If they were easy, then someone smarter than me in this job before me would have already done them." Too many politicians and interest groups propose solutions that are "easy," or "costless," when they're anything but. Too often the ability of government, particularly federally, to "solve" a problem is overstated. And when a solution is promised that doesn't work so easily, quickly or simply or deliver a promised outcome, this further reduces public faith and trust. Surely one of the lessons has to be not to constantly ramp up the promises, but to be honest about the limits of government and the speed with which the promised solutions can be achieved. But again, the new media environment makes 140-character promises easier to campaign on than complex explanations of why they won't work.

Scott Ryan

Delivery Address:
LEVEL 1, 221 DRUMMOND ST
CARLTON VIC 3053

No stamp required
if posted in Australia

Quarterly Essay
REPLY PAID 90094
CARLTON VIC 3053

Delivery Address:
LEVEL 1, 221 DRUMMOND ST
CARLTON VIC 3053

No stamp required
if posted in Australia

Quarterly Essay
REPLY PAID 90094
CARLTON VIC 3053

FOLLOW
THE
LEADER

Correspondence

Sean Kelly

Laura Tingle, in order to point to the structural changes to the presidency that Donald Trump may leave behind, helpfully cites Miranda Carter on Kaiser Wilhelm II. Carter argues that the Kaiser had certain odd personality traits, which found sympathy in Germany during his reign, but which left the nation depleted after his abdication.

Of course, as Carter's description makes clear, both men can rightly be called egotistical fools. We can hold them in contempt, but holding them personally responsible for the deep wounds they might open is another matter.

But what of our current batch of political leaders in Australia? Think of them what you like, they are sane and capable of complex thought. Their attacks on democracy are not so strident. The legacy these attacks will leave is not really structural; it is emotional. It is still a legacy.

Now that prime ministers are removed with alacrity, we can easily forget the specific beginnings of the current period of tumult. There were several factors behind Kevin Rudd's removal, but one was the importation of a model that had seemed to work, up to a point, in New South Wales. One of the very great mistakes in this was the assumption that a prime minister was just like a premier – when the relationship between voters and the leader of the nation is very different from that between voters and the leader of a state. Premiers are important, but I suspect a prime minister affects the way we think about our own identity in a way a premier never will. The move was self-fulfilling: by treating a prime minister like a premier, a course was embarked upon which leads us to the place where we now find ourselves, in which prime ministers have in fact been reduced almost to the status of premiers.

The point, an obvious one, though not quite so obvious at the time, is that actions taken to preserve power in the short term can end up having long-term effects. Again, leadership change is not the only factor in the rapid escalation in disrespect for politicians and government, but few would suggest it has not been a major one.

This put me in mind of more recent and more minor examples, which are still, I believe, important. The new – at the time of writing – prime minister, Scott Morrison, has already, in just under two months, made several comments that seem dismissive of the job he has taken on and the institutions that surround him.

He began by talking about the "Muppet show" around the removal of Malcolm Turnbull. The diagnosis was fair, but in making it – presumably in an eagerness to empathise with voters – he overlooked, perhaps, the authority a prime minister's words still, against all odds, have. The leader of one of the country's two major parties describing his party in that way does nothing to restore respect.

Not long after, the prime minister cancelled a Council of Australian Governments (COAG) meeting, which was expected to deal with school and hospital funding. The move was understandable; a new prime minister may well want to alter arrangements. But at a press conference he was asked a bland question about the status of various meetings and took the opportunity to attack Labor, with the risk of casting aspersions on COAG itself: "The Labor Party can have as many meetings as they like, they [don't] seem to be able to resolve anything when they are in government. They were great at having meetings. The only thing that happens as a result of not having that COAG meeting is less Tim Tams will be consumed in Canberra that week."

More recently, Mr Morrison was asked by Alan Jones about the conclusions of the IPCC's latest climate change report. Again, he chose to go on the attack on something he had not even been asked about: "No, we're not held to any of them at all, Alan, nor are we bound to go and tip money into that big climate fund, we're not going to do that either. So I'm not going to spend money on global climate conferences and all that sort of nonsense, I'm not going to get in there . . . "

In the space of a few weeks, the prime minister sought to ridicule his own party, federal–state governance and international governance. Then there was his threat to intervene at the ABC: "I expect the ABC board to do better. And if they don't, well they can expect a bit more attention from me."

There is no mystery about this approach. In a 2017 address to the Liberal Party federal council, Morrison, then the treasurer, talked about the appeal of Donald Trump and Jeremy Corbyn, who, he said, had taken "on the role of the authentic outsider; challenging a system that many voters did not think was serving them any longer." In other words, our prime minister is borrowing from the strongman's playbook.

Lack of civility is a related issue. Tingle mentions, in passing, Bill Shorten's use of "Turnbull" instead of "Mr Turnbull." Shorten and Morrison have each used "this guy" to describe the other. In that federal council speech, Morrison said this of Shorten: "It's no coincidence his initials are BS."

There is reasonable political thinking behind all this. Morrison wishes to present himself as the practically minded outsider, focused on action not meetings. Neither man wishes to accord respect to his opposite number. But this is the point: what are seen as short-term political gains – with rhetoric as the main weapon – increasingly come at the expense of respect for politicians and government. You cannot tear down an institution you are leading, or want to lead, without ultimately being yourself weakened.

The reckless use of rhetoric is not limited to government. Tingle rightly points to the fading influence of other voices that once held authority in national debates, such as religious organisations and business. Here, too, we can observe the deleterious effect of crazily antagonistic words. I am reminded of businesses railing against the political instability of the past few years, seemingly forgetting their own starring role: the ferocity with which they sought to destroy a carbon price and a mining tax, and the leaders behind those policies. I am also reminded of the more recent scaremongering from Catholic schools over new funding proposals, their attempts to mislead voters and parents.

Tingle ends her essay calling for national leaders to help rebuild the national debate. It is a worthy hope. There is an open question as to whether it is possible, for at least two reasons. The first is that the rhetoric of both politicians and stakeholders is driven partly by the desire to cut through an increasingly noisy public sphere. The volume and tempo of media seems unlikely to drop. I might want these groups to moderate their rhetoric, but if their voice is not being heard then the temptation to yell will remain.

The second is the possibility that voters are no longer listening to leaders, experts and institutions because they believe the world is fundamentally broken – and if those groups haven't led us here, who has? The analysis and its attendant suspicions may not be entirely fair – but then again, they might be. You don't have to be a conspiracy theorist to agree that there is a kind of club of those who hold formal authority in this and other countries – and that the rules by which those in the club operate have not always been helpful to those outside the club. I agree that a civil and intelligent national debate is essential. But if "rebuilding" is, or is perceived to be, an attempt to build again what was there before, then it is likely to fail, and perhaps deservedly so.

Sean Kelly

FOLLOW THE LEADER

Correspondence

Amanda McKenzie

"We have all read about the great figures of history, and that reading shapes our view of what makes a true leader," Laura Tingle writes early in *Follow the Leader*.

The great leaders of history, written up in university textbooks and glorified in movies, tend to be Anglo-Saxon men in positions of political power. Perhaps in looking for these "great leaders" today, we're actually missing the leadership emerging all around us.

Leaders are pretty easy to spot: there are people following them. And by following, I don't mean voting. I mean going some place together: a movement. As Tingle describes, strong leadership involves building consensus across the community to deal with complex challenges.

It has been quite a while since anyone in political power was a real leader of a vibrant movement. That doesn't mean there aren't strong leaders and vibrant movements today, but they seem absent from Tingle's piece.

The #MeToo movement is shaking the foundations of power and entitlement, driven by a deeply authentic and decentralised wave of leadership from across the world. If anyone doubts it is a legitimate movement, consider this. The measure of a movement is that it allows participants to do together what they would never be able to do alone. Sharing stories of harassment and assault is an incredibly brave thing to do, and speaks to the deep level of solidarity #MeToo has built. Further, #MeToo has rapidly shifted community understanding and given some of the worst perpetrators their comeuppance. Individuals are demonstrating the sort of leadership, authenticity and bravery that we would love to see from politicians.

The marriage equality debate catalysed a similar movement. Politicians, too many of them late and convenient supporters, celebrated the successful vote in parliament. But true leadership belonged to LGBTIQ people across the country, whose honesty and courage persuaded voters around Australia.

The decentralised leadership in these examples is quite different to traditional positional leadership. It comes from authenticity. See, for example, the Parkland students' enormous capacity for influence following a shooting at their school. The students were clearer and more convincing than many established gun-reform activists, who have consistently blunted their own language with political pragmatism and message-testing.

The most effective organisations working on social issues today often put their resources into elevating the emerging authentic voices of those directly affected by an issue – for instance, the groups that supported the Parkland students to run the #NeverAgain rallies. This leadership is the opposite of a centralised model of elevating one brand or spokesperson.

Tingle argues that voices at the community level – scientists, business leaders, community groups – are taken less seriously than in the past. This may be the attitude of political parties and the press gallery, but the examples above demonstrate the exact opposite when it comes to the public. Many activist and charity organisations now have email lists and social-media profiles that give them serious potential to lead and persuade audiences. The best organisations create content that their base shares with its own networks, enhancing credibility and building a broader audience.

Of course, community movements are not new. What is striking is how disconnected our political debate is from them.

Why are we not seeing leadership from our politicians?

As Tingle points out, the electorate is rarely the most important constituency for politicians. The first priority of a parliamentary leader is to secure their position within their party – that means caucus, factions, donors, media moguls and other vested interests. Satisfying these interests, rather than the interests of voters, is part of the reason why the major political parties often seem so out of touch with the Australian public. Getting vested interests out of politics through political donation reform is critical. For instance, entrenched coal interests have made tackling climate change at a federal level impossible, as Malcolm Turnbull admitted on his exit. Unless that changes, how can we expect our politics to play out any differently?

As Tingle argues, over the last decade or so it seems that a unifying commitment to a central purpose has unravelled. Neither party has a significant public membership, and there seems to be no interest in fostering one. That means our major political parties are without the anchor of a direct link to the community beyond the news cycle and elections.

However, to be fair to our politicians, theirs is an incredibly hard and thankless job. Many are good people in very challenging circumstances. Tingle notes that "Complex change ... requires more political time and space than we seem prepared to give our leaders." Politicians travel at least half the year; senior figures are constantly responding to the media cycle and rarely have an uninterrupted weekend or holiday. After leaving federal politics, former environment minister Greg Combet noted he had been working eighteen-hour days for seven days a week for years.

Tingle canvasses other increased demands – from following every sporting code to having a ready response to the broad array of foreign policy challenges. There seems to be an expectation on the one hand that politicians are just "like us," watching the World Cup into the wee hours. On the other, they are required to be superhuman, able to have a thoughtful, immediate view on all the complex issues of the day (which must be the same view as that of all their colleagues).

Remember when Julia Gillard was mocked for failing to have any fruit in her fruit bowl in 2005? I suspect most senior politicians, like senior business leaders, are doing very little shopping and cooking at home. But contempt for politicians is sport in Australia, and there is little empathy for how difficult and demanding it must be. The adrenaline-fuelled nature of political debate – a constant state of fight or flight – leaves little space for reflection. Interestingly, one of the effects of long-term exposure to heightened adrenaline is that the brain becomes more focused on a narrow field, and capacity for compassion and empathy is diminished.

Journalists, similarly, have little time to go beyond personalities to substance. Shrinking newsrooms, the decline of special subject-matter reporters and a demanding 24-hour media cycle means the fourth estate is more focused on the narrow field of political machinations. All this tells us that the lack of substantive leadership Tingle describes is structural. Tingle laments the lack of contemporary political personalities like Paul Keating, but would his approach have been successful in the current environment?

Where will leadership come from?

The leadership crisis Tingle describes is structural, but the solutions she articulates focus on individual behaviour, rather than the environment in which those individuals act. For instance, journalists should "think often and hard" about what they cover, and politicians should stop shooting the messenger. Asking individuals to be more courageous or responsible is insufficient. It's hard to change the players unless we change the rules. It also assumes that most politicians share the larger goal of preserving the valued institutions of our democracy even when this is at the expense of "winning" the daily news cycle.

Perhaps the kind of strong leadership Tingle describes is now less likely to come from classic positional leadership. What we need are political leaders who will effectively follow and enhance community movements, rather than the other way around. Tingle gives the example of Lyndon Johnston, who harnessed the momentum of the civil-rights movement to foster political change. We don't need politicians to be "stronger leaders" so much as we need them to be wiser followers.

The most recent example Tingle offers of an attempt at consensus-building is Malcolm Turnbull's National Energy Guarantee (NEG). The policy itself was enormously cynical: it would make no positive difference to the issues it claimed to address. It was a policy to reduce emissions that would see pollution increase. A policy to tackle energy prices which would bring on less new supply than doing nothing at all. To the extent that people were persuaded, it was only that they were so worn down by more than a decade of torturous politics. However, ultimately the lack of consensus within the Coalition killed the policy.

Public polling consistently shows that the vast majority of Australians want action on climate change. Similarly, most of us prefer renewable energy to coal and understand that large and small batteries will be critical to Australia's energy future. Most big-business leaders now want action, as do stakeholders, from the Australian Medical Association to the National Farmers' Federation. There are strong community campaigns against the Adani mine. Little, if any, of this latent community power could be mobilised for the NEG. However, as the drought bites, the Great Barrier Reef suffers extreme mortality rates from bleaching and we experience worsening heatwaves, the politics will change. One place to begin is by challenging the influence of vested interests in our politics, starting with donations reform.

To conclude, though, I will leave you with the questions I was left pondering after finishing Tingle's essay. First, what are the conditions that would facilitate strong community leadership in Australia, and strong followers in our parliamentarians? And second, what will it take for those conditions to become the operating environment for Australian politics?

Amanda McKenzie

FOLLOW THE LEADER

Correspondence

Shireen Morris

"Why would you want to go into politics?"

I've been standing at train stations the past several weeks, handing out flyers in my fingerless gloves. Shivering in the morning sun. Saying hello to commuters.

This is a new experience. I've been an actor, a singer, a check-out chick and an admin assistant. A constitutional lawyer and an advocate. Never a unionist, a staffer or a wannabe politician. Never a campaigner on the street. The hustings, as they say, is an exciting new place.

A sample of the flustered public rushes by, half of them blocking me out with earphones, iPhones and well-planned head-down avoidance of eye contact (I don't blame them) – but others are eager to chat. Among the occasional "Well done!" and complaints about the Liberal leadership spill, the "I'm not voting for a Dutton man!" declarations and the bread-and-butter questions about healthcare, schools, wages and penalty rates, plus the odd "Piss off, you're all the same!" reprimand, people also occasionally pause to ask: "Why on earth would you want to go into politics?"

The disillusionment underlying the question is palpable. Politicians are liars and backstabbers, seems to be the view. "It's a dirty game. They're just in it for themselves," people observe. And given the machinations of recent times, they appear to be right. "Do you think you can really make a difference?" one local asks, genuinely wanting to know. My answer is, as usual, "I hope I can. I will work hard to." But people are fed up with self-serving politicians. They have every right to be sceptical.

As the new Labor candidate for Deakin, I found that Laura Tingle's Quarterly Essay posed a bracing question: what are the characteristics of a true leader, and what is true leadership in politics? And why did I think I could, or should, put myself forward to represent my community – this particular part of the eastern suburbs of Melbourne where I grew up – in federal parliament?

The bullying and backstabbing that seem to characterise contemporary Australian politics raise a further question: why would a woman strive to be a politician in today's climate? And if parts of society now crave a "strongman," as Tingle contends, how does one strive to be a strong woman in a political system that is not only male-dominated, but also increasingly vitriolic, vengeful and polarised?

Is it possible to be better than the existing culture, or even to change that culture for the better? Within this system, can one be not only a good politician, but also a good leader?

An experienced parliamentarian, offering advice on my campaign, observed that Parliament has many consummate politicians – people who can talk well, play the game and appear polished. "But Parliament needs more thoughtful people," he said. This set a nice challenge. Don't just be a slick politician. Be thoughtful. Be a leader.

I tend towards optimism, so I believe Australia's democratic culture can change for the better. It requires the Australian people, and the politicians themselves, to insist things change. To demand it.

I largely agree with Tingle's stated criteria for a good leader. Leaders should explain, advocate and persuade people to adopt good ideas. *Follow the Leader* discussed the former US president Lyndon Johnson. Noel Pearson also often talks about LBJ's strategic prowess, and the way he seized a historic moment to deliver the *Civil Rights Act* in the face of tough conditions. LBJ was a great persuader. I watched the movie *All the Way*, which dramatises his civil rights strategy, and was struck by a key line. Johnson's advisers were trying to warn him that pursuing Kennedy's civil rights bill could jeopardise his electoral chances. "What the hell's the presidency for?" LBJ demanded. He stuck to his guns. The *Civil Rights Act* was signed into law in 1964.

Tingle is correct that leaders must know how to seize historic opportunities. Instead, we often see politicians baulking at leading necessary reform, in favour of playing it safe at the polls. Clinging to power, instead of wielding it for the national good. In doing so, they too often underestimate the people.

One of my frustrations working as an advocate for Indigenous constitutional recognition has been the way some politicians blame the public for their lack of reform action. In rejecting the Uluru Statement from the Heart, Malcolm Turnbull not only verballed the Australian people – he blamed them for his cowardly stance. A First Nations voice in the constitution is not "desirable or capable of winning acceptance at referendum," Turnbull claimed. "The government does not believe such a radical change to our constitution's representative institutions has any realistic prospect of being supported by a majority of Australians in a majority of states."

When asked if the government had evidence to back this up, Indigenous Affairs Minister Nigel Scullion said they had done no polling – he was just "following his gut." The Australian people were used an excuse for government inaction, but with no evidence. These so-called leaders chose to pessimistically predict that Australians would reject a First Nations voice, instead of just asking them – through a referendum.

Polling exposed the dishonesty of the Liberal government's excuse. An Omnipoll showed 61 per cent of Australians would vote yes to a First Nations Voice in the Constitution – and that was in the face of government opposition. Does that figure sound familiar? It's the same proportion that voted "yes" in the same-sex marriage postal survey.

On same-sex marriage, Turnbull, despite his procedural incompetence, at least advocated for the reform. "Lucy and I will be voting yes," he said. With such leadership, Australians voted 61 per cent in favour. He showed no such leadership on Indigenous recognition. On this issue, Turnbull was a deliberate wet blanket and even promulgated lies about the proposal, calling it a "third chamber of parliament."

The proposal is not a "third chamber" and not "radical" – and Turnbull knew it. In 2015, in a private meeting, Turnbull (then communications minister) told Noel Pearson and me that an Indigenous advisory body in the Constitution "sounds sensible" and even offered to help promote it, perhaps through a pub event in Wentworth. A few years later, as prime minister, he fearmongered. My best explanation is that he caved in to pressure from the right of his party in order to cling to his position.

Yet what is the prime ministership for, if not for Indigenous constitutional recognition?

Paul Keating understood the importance of reconciliation for the soul and future of our nation. Perhaps Turnbull, deep down, understood it too. In 2011, he reflected on the history of colonisation in Melbourne in *The Monthly*:

> When governments say doing the right thing is "too hard," what they are really saying is that it is more lucrative, or expedient, to do the wrong thing. Our forebears preached protection of native people and the blessings of Christ while they largely destroyed a people and a way of life.
>
> So if you ever walk quietly along Robert Hoddle's wide boulevards or along the banks of the Yarra, tamed to look like an English

> river, listen carefully. You may hear the weeping of the Kulin – betrayed, dispossessed, but not yet quite forgotten.

Yet in 2017, faced with the political realities within his party, Turnbull rejected the Uluru Statement. Doing the right thing was evidently too hard. It was more expedient to do the wrong thing.

It takes a leader with both moral courage and strategic nous to achieve substantive reconciliatory reform – especially constitutional reform, which requires the support of both left and right. I'm not saying it's easy. One, of course, must compromise and rally consensus. One must keep power in order to use it.

Yet after capitulating to internal right-wing detractors on many important policies and principles, Turnbull still got knifed. The lesson is clear: selling out does not necessarily stop insurrection. It only shows you don't stand for anything.

The same-sex marriage survey demonstrated that many Liberal Party politicians are often behind the Australian electorate on matters of social justice. The Liberal Party insisted on the postal survey. But Tony Abbott, an elected representative of the Australian people, did not respect his own electorate's wishes. Although Warringah voted 75 per cent in favour of same-sex marriage, Abbott left the parliamentary chamber before the final vote on the legislation, along with his conservative colleague, Michael Sukkar. Sukkar had promised he would respect the outcome of the survey and respect his electorate's wishes. His electorate, Deakin, voted 65.7 per cent in favour – also above the national average. Yet Sukkar ran out of the Parliamentary Chamber behind Abbott when the final vote was imminent.

What does this say about how connected the right wing of the Liberal Party are to their democratic constituents? Refusing to listen to Australians you represent – that is not leadership. Breaking a promise to respect the electorate's wishes – that is not leadership. Running out of the Chamber – that is not leadership.

The best leaders, when dealing with vexing policy and political problems, take on board the legitimate concerns of their opponents, learn from them and use the lessons to forge a new and better synthesis position. They hammer out a noble compromise. When I say noble compromise, I do not mean a lowest common denominator compromise. It is possible to find a noble compromise on persisting disagreements.

Finding this "radical centre" requires both parties to shift. To shift one's position, even if slightly, shows humility. It also shows intelligence – for the smartest people know they cannot be right on everything, and even their rightness can be refined. The insights of others, bringing different life experiences to our own, can open our minds – if only we have the courage to hear what others say. It also shows empathy. Listening to and acknowledging opposing views lets others know their grievances have been heard. Feeling heard is conducive to cohesion, inclusion and unity.

Tingle is correct, I think, that a huge part of leadership is the ability to corral opposing factions into compromise agreements, both within one's own party and within the broader parliament, but also across the public sphere. This is also the way to create good policy. The best policy is not simply that of the left or right. The best policy synthesises the brilliance that can be found across the political spectrum, and across the breadth of philosophical thought: good ideas from socialism, liberalism and conservatism. The Liberal Party's slide to the right demonstrates a loss of balanced leadership, and this is bad for Australia. Politics needs balance, not extremism.

"Why would you want to become a politician?"

When Malcolm Turnbull rejected the Uluru Statement, I, like so many Australians, was heartbroken. A historic, unprecedented First Nations consensus was ignored. Years of lobbying from the outside came to nothing. I realised then that you have to be inside parliament, where the decisions are made, to truly change things – and not just on constitutional reform, but on climate change, health, education, inequality and so much more.

The events of the past several months, and indeed the leadership instability of the past several years, pose a challenge to politicians and would-be politicians – on all sides. Our democracy needs to do better. My hope is that political representatives can find ways to pursue leadership in the inclusive and intelligent centre, to focus more on the best policy and the best ideas, and less on plotting and "playing the game." The challenge for all of us is to work together to herald the better angels of our nation's nature.

Shireen Morris

FOLLOW THE LEADER

Correspondence

Dennis Atkins

Barack Obama was a great US president who might one day gain the recognition he deserves, but for now he's in the crossfire of contemporary politics. He has been unfairly criticised for what people call his dithering on international relations. Current president Donald Trump uses Obama as a punching bag – when he's not urging crowds to shout that Hillary Clinton should be locked up. However, any serious look at Obama's time in the White House – an extraordinary period, from the height of the Great Recession, through the catching and killing of Osama bin Laden and into difficult domestic arguments about massive issues such as national healthcare reform – will surely come down on the positive.

Laura Tingle's brilliant essay on modern leadership skips through the last three hundred years of leaders, from Abraham Lincoln and Franklin Delano Roosevelt to the giant Lyndon Baines Johnson, before landing in the modern era. It's the best of Tingle's three Quarterly Essays and needs a postscript on what is coming next. Is the strongman – the Trump White House, Putin in Russia, Xi in Beijing, Erdoğan in Turkey, Sisi in Cairo, the House of Saud in Riyadh, Duterte in the Philippines and the looming ascension of Jair Bolsonaro in Brazil – here to stay, or will there be a return to more centrist democracy? We need this considered and answered.

More fundamentally, we should review Obama's leadership from 2009 to 2017. Going back to one of his foundation speeches that was praised and then, sadly, brushed aside, Obama laid down markers for a new international policy when, in June 2009, he addressed students in Cairo and called for a new compact between the United States and the global Muslim population.

"I've come here to Cairo to seek a new beginning between the United States and Muslims," he said, adding that the two populations shared overlapping, common principles "of justice and progress; tolerance and the dignity of all human beings." The president went on to address religious freedom, one of the most divisive issues when the clashes between great religions and civilisations are laid bare. "Islam has a proud tradition of tolerance," said Obama:

> We see it in the history of Andalusia and Cordoba during the Inquisition. I saw it firsthand as a child in Indonesia, where devout Christians worshipped freely in an overwhelmingly Muslim country. That is the spirit we need today.
>
> People in every country should be free to choose and live their faith based upon the persuasion of the mind and the heart and the soul. This tolerance is essential for religion to thrive, but it's being challenged in many different ways.
>
> Among some Muslims, there's a disturbing tendency to measure one's own faith by the rejection of somebody else's faith. The richness of religious diversity must be upheld – whether it is for Maronites in Lebanon or the Copts in Egypt. And ... fault lines must be closed among Muslims, as well, as the divisions between Sunni and Shia have led to tragic violence, particularly in Iraq.

By any measure, Obama was charting a new course that demanded global attention, but it went without the follow-up necessary, either from the then new president or from Islamic nations around the world. Soon it was being labelled the first of Obama's so-called missed opportunities. But was it really his fault? I'd say not.

Obama was perhaps naive in thinking the old, autocratic rulers of the Middle East were going to give way to a more democratic, perhaps even liberal, way of doing things. From Cairo to Tripoli and eventually to Damascus, it all went to custard. But Obama can't really be marked down too harshly for this – just about all of the Western intelligentsia and many Western governments were on this "Arab Spring" bus. His one big mistake, which he still tosses and turns in his mind, was the laying down of a "red line" in Syria: a nerve-gas line that the brutal dictator Bashar Hafez al-Assad was only too ready to cross and make his population suffer even more. Obama didn't respond as he should have (and as Trump did years later) and he has paid the price in history's story.

This might be a black mark for Obama, but let's have a close look at perhaps the biggest decision that's been taken by a US president in decades: the killing of Osama bin Laden. This was not a slam dunk. It was a 50/50 call at best, based on the best available intelligence. The United States knew there was a compound, near Pakistani military facilities, where a tall Arab walked about outside, behind a very high wall. Those in the compound burnt all their rubbish and were secretive in their comings and goings, but without any face-to-face identification no one could be 100 per cent sure it was bin Laden in there.

As the call went around the room, Vice President Joe Biden was against a strike, as was Defence Secretary Bill Gates, while Secretary of State Hillary Clinton thought a missile was justified. Obama turned to his trusted foreign policy adviser Ben Rhodes, asking him what he thought. "You were always going to make this decision," said Rhodes, having watched his boss stare without blinking for many minutes. They killed the man who, on the morning of 11 September 2001, orchestrated the death of almost 3000 people, when deadly planes came out of the clear blue sky.

This was a brave move – one of great courage and import, which could have gone horribly wrong if it had not been correct. Obama might have made some wobbly moves and decisions in foreign policy, but you can never take away from him this clear-eyed go-ahead for the strike on bin Laden. The world is a better place for what he did.

Elsewhere, Obama was the president who did what many of his predecessors tried to do and failed – he introduced a form of universal healthcare against fierce opposition. Democrat giant LBJ didn't do it, despite getting his "Great Society" package into law, while Republican Richard Nixon made an effort, working with Democrat Edward "Teddy" Kennedy, without success. The next to push the big rock up the hill was Hillary Clinton, working on behalf of her husband, President Bill Clinton. It was Obama who got it across the line and, despite some undoing by Trump, it remains largely intact.

Obama was a substantial and consequential president, although he might not be regarded as transformative – the goal he had set for himself. We can blame the times for that, as much as mistakes made in the White House. One thing he did do was leave us with perhaps the greatest set of presidential speeches heard in more than a century. We await his next memoir with joyful anticipation.

Dennis Atkins

FOLLOW THE LEADER

Correspondence

Nyadol Nyuon

"We hold these truths to be self-evident, that all men are created equal, that they are endowed by their Creator with certain unalienable Rights, that among these are Life, Liberty and the pursuit of Happiness." Thomas Jefferson's oft-quoted words, from the Declaration of Independence, continue to inspire many today; however, they were written by men who "participated in the brutal and degrading institution of slavery."

In his book *Less Than Human*, David Livingstone Smith writes that in light of Jefferson's participation in the institution of slavery, his words in the Declaration raised the question who "should be counted as human." And to "square the moral circle" between the "economic attraction of slavery and the Enlightenment vision of human dignity," the Founding Father of the American Republic found a way by denying that African slaves were human. This view was shared by many "champions of liberty" at the time, and such views continued to be enshrined in laws and administered by democratic institutions (such as the US Supreme Court) until the civil rights movements of the 1950s and 1960s.

While the Founding Fathers and Enlightenment thinkers might have reconciled their apparent inconsistencies, the words of the Declaration never had the power to persuade the likes of Frederick Douglass, a former slave and abolitionist. In a speech delivered seventy-six years later, he invoked the Declaration to point to the hypocrisy embedded in America from the time of its founding. He described what the anniversary of independence meant to African slaves in America:

> I am not included within the pale of this glorious anniversary! Your high independence only reveals the immeasurable distance between us. The blessings in which you this day rejoice, are not enjoyed in common …
>
> What, to the American slave, is your 4th of July? I answer; a day that reveals to him, more than all other days in the year, the gross

> injustice and cruelty to which he is the constant victim. To him, your celebration is a sham; your boasted liberty, an unholy license; your national greatness, swelling vanity; your sound of rejoicing are [sic] empty and heartless; your denunciations of tyrants brass fronted impudence; your shouts of liberty and equality, hollow mockery; your prayers and hymns, your sermons and thanksgivings, with all your religious parade and solemnity, are to him, mere bombast, fraud, deception, impiety, and hypocrisy – a thin veil to cover up crimes which would disgrace a nation of savages.

These are strong words, but appropriate for their time.

What, though, does the Declaration of Independence have to do with an essay about political leadership in the modern world? The simple answer is that the inconsistencies and hypocrisies that existed at that time are an inherent part of Western democracies – at least as viewed by those who have never fully enjoyed democracy's fruits.

Those inconsistencies and hypocrisies, arguably, still exist today. "When was it ever great?" was one African American reply to Donald Trump's campaign slogan "Make America Great Again." Some of the issues discussed in Laura Tingle's essay, such as the apparent failure of democracy and its links to the rise of the "strongman" leader, would not be new to certain groups of people, because even if leaders with strongman personas did not exist, they were governed in ways that mirrored strongmen politics and tactics.

It has been argued, for example, that, "the relationship between the American democratic government and African Americans is analogous to the totalitarian power hierarchy. The U.S. government bears a resemblance to elites while African Americans resemble the ruled class in the totalitarian power structure." On that view, Donald Trump is a new incarnation of an old type.

That said, there might be a difference that explains the reaction of moderate Americans to Trump. The possible difference is that there has been an expansion of the category of scapegoat – in the Trump era, moderate and liberal Americans and political opponents are now targeted alongside more traditional scapegoat groups, such as African Americans, other minorities and foreigners.

Tingle quotes Steven Levitsky and Daniel Ziblatt, from their book *How Democracies Die*:

> Republican politicians … learned that in a polarized society, treating rivals as enemies can be useful – and that the pursuit of politics as warfare can mobilize people who fear they have much to lose.

The labelling of political opponents and others as scapegoats changes the conduct of politics (by "rewriting the rules of politics to permanently disadvantage" rivals) and of leaders (all the way from Newt Gingrich to Donald Trump).

Nikki Haley, the outgoing US ambassador to the United Nations, denied this applied to the United States recently, when she said:

> In our toxic political environment, I've heard some people in both parties describe their opponents as enemies or evil. In America, our political opponents are not evil. In South Sudan, where rape is routinely used as a weapon of war – that is evil. In Syria, where the dictator uses chemical weapons to murder innocent children – that is evil. In North Korea, where American student Otto Warmbier was tortured to death – that was evil. In the last two years, I've seen true evil.

Haley's statement reveals the inconsistency and hypocrisy of American democracy. While the United States holds itself up as democratic, better and greater than other nations, a close look at recent American history, domestic and foreign, would produce a list of "evils" to rival those given by Haley: the use of torture in the War on Terror; the indefinite detention without trial of prisoners at Guantanamo; the killing, rape, torture and humiliation suffered by prisoners at Abu Ghraib prison during the Iraq War; or the recent Trump policy to separate immigrant children from their parents and relatives at the US border.

Some of the examples above relate to American foreign policy, and I accept Laura Tingle's view that foreign policy is a different area of leadership. Tingle, however, acknowledges that how foreign policy is conducted can influence domestic politics. It can change "the way we see and judge our leaders" and has been used by political leaders to "escape the obligation to consult and build a consensus – whether to pursue actions they believe in on the world stage, or to present themselves as strong leaders at home."

Perhaps in addition, the conduct of foreign policy (and the way we treat minorities or "enemies" within) influences our domestic politics in more insidious ways. The War on Terror has possibly transformed Western democracies as it has transformed countries such as Afghanistan and Iraq. It shifts the "Overton Window" by expanding what it is acceptable for leaders to do in the domestic sphere. In my view, one of the ways this occurs is by gradually eroding belief in the importance and the indispensability of principles and norms that were once held to be fundamental to how a society saw itself. One wonders, for example, whether the reported abuses against American citizens under the *Patriot Act* would have occurred without the War on Terror. A report in 2007 showed the FBI was "increasingly targeting citizens and green card holders, with more than 11,517 requests in 2006 targeting U.S. persons, while Non-U.S. persons were targeted with 8,605 requests."

In 1852, Frederick Douglass registered how the treatment of those deemed to be enemies, and therefore deserving of hostile treatment, could corrupt all. In his speech, he asserted that the existence of slavery "destroys your moral power abroad; it corrupts your politicians at home."

In another, related context, David Smith emphasised that one would be "sorely mistaken" to think of rhetoric dehumanising others as mere talk. He argued: "Dehumanization isn't a way of talking. It's a way of thinking ... It acts as a psychological lubricant, dissolving our inhibitions and inflaming our destructive passions. As such, it empowers us to perform acts that would, under other circumstances, be unthinkable."

Like the author, I have zoomed out a little further than "Trumpian political developments" to the underlying subject of the essay: how do we best organise a community of people? The answer will depend in part on who is considered part of the community and therefore who is consulted, listened to and protected. I have argued that because certain groups have never enjoyed the full benefits of living in democracies, and have in fact been the direct victims of strongmen politics even as their societies claimed to be democratic, there is, in fact, no slide to some more worrying type of political leader, nor is there a crisis of democracy – at least not one justifying the current reaction.

In their 2014 article "The Crisis of Democracy: Which Crisis? Which Democracy?" Selen A. Ercan and Jean-Paul Gagnon argued, "there is nothing new about the democratic crisis diagnosis. In other words, crisis has never been the exception to the rule; rather, it is an inherent feature of democracy ... [yet] if crisis is an inherent feature of democratic politics ... what we need is a more reflexive democracy – a type of democracy that continuously confronts its own limits and logics of exclusion." That democracy is not a settled concept is revealed in terms such as "the American experiment," or in President Macron's statement that "France, the country of revolution, is once again a leading political laboratory."

Conceivably, a good place to start in understanding how to confront the limits and logic of exclusion in a democracy is the essay's recommendation that leaders have to rebuild "the national political discussion after years of it being under assault." Perhaps by doing so they can foster an environment that does more for democracy than "keep the word of promise to our ear, and break it to our hope."

Nyadol Nyuon

FOLLOW THE LEADER

Correspondence

Norman Abjorensen

Democracy is in crisis. The rise of the political strongman is very much a part of the crisis, but rather than being a cause, it is merely a symptom of a much wider malaise in which democracy everywhere is under siege.

As long as democracy has existed, it has been a fragile creature: seldom secure, always assailed. Throughout history, the strongman – a political actor who seeks to rule by force and brooks no opposition – has lurked in the shadows wherever democracy has emerged. The strongman is the ultimate political stalker, and has always found support among those who feel threatened by any tendency to shift power from the few to the many.

The study of democratisation, so beloved by American political scientists in the later twentieth century as evidence that the world was becoming more like the United States, has all too often downplayed that the process is always a coin with two sides: the masses who seek to gain on the one side; the oligarchs or plutocrats, who were previously both entrenched and privileged, on the other. Resistance is inevitable, if not to stop democratisation altogether, then at least to limit its effects.

While democratisation was earlier viewed as a phenomenon largely confined to the developing world, especially recently decolonised states, it was later extended to the study of states emerging from dictatorship and military rule, and later still to those states in Eastern Europe and Central Asia that had been under Soviet domination. However, even in developed states where democracy was thought to have taken root and cultivated sturdy institutions, democratisation was seen first to stall, then to go into reverse.

This phenomenon was termed "autocratisation" – a concept popularised by researchers in the Varieties of Democracy project at the University of Gothenburg, Sweden – which denotes a measurable decline in democratic qualities; that is, democratisation in reverse. According to Professor Staffan Lindberg, autocratisation can be seen as a process in which democratic institutions, rights and practices are curtailed or undermined – to the point where an autocratic regime may take hold. Autocratisation affects mainly non-electoral aspects of democracy, such as media freedom, freedom of expression and the rule of law, yet these in turn threaten to undermine the meaningfulness of elections.

While autocrats such as Russia's Vladimir Putin have come to power in a country lacking a viable democratic heritage and institutions, creeping autocratisation may be seen in states that for a time showed a strong democratic trajectory, such as Poland and Hungary. Certainly, in Turkey, which has had a mixed record of democratic experiment since the modernising efforts of Kemal Atatürk a century ago, the current trend under the strongman Recep Tayyip Erdoğan is very much in the direction of autocratisation. It might even be argued that the United States under Donald Trump exhibits certain autocratic tendencies.

Early last century, feeble attempts at establishing democracies in Italy and Germany were crushed by emerging strongmen, most famously in the form of Benito Mussolini and Adolf Hitler, but they were only the best known. Elsewhere in Europe, notably in Spain, Portugal, Hungary, Poland, Romania, Greece and the Baltic states, powerful coalitions of vested interests, including industrialists, landholders and, in Catholic countries, the Church, fought against democratic advance to protect their feudal privileges. In Japan, emerging democratic elements, including the adoption of universal male suffrage in 1928 and competing political parties, were similarly reversed as the military and traditional aristocracy reasserted their grip on power. By 1942, with much of the world locked in military conflict, democracy was a flickering flame in a hurricane, with the number of democracies down to a mere twelve.

It is worth asking the question: whose interests do strongmen serve? It is as relevant now as it was in the interwar period of the twentieth century. The spread of national self-determination and democracy after World War I, fanned by the idealism of US President Woodrow Wilson, threatened the old order already shaken by the fall of the old empires and the rise of the Bolsheviks in Russia. Mussolini saw his mission as opposing the degenerate idea of political democracy and restoring the glories of ancient Rome; Hitler similarly revelled in the fantasy of a mythical, racially pure Germany; Franco, in Spain, for his part, sought to defend the aristocracy and the Church from an assault by the common people. At the heart of their opposition was the wholesale rejection of the very notion of political equality, a fundamental precept of democracy.

Equality was at the core of the first flowering of democracy, in ancient Athens. Pericles, in his famous Funeral Oration in 431 BCE, offered a concise definition of Athenian democracy and its key characteristics, emphasising that equality was fundamental. The Greeks coined a term, "isonomia" (Greek: ἰσονομία), meaning, broadly, the principle of political equality for all, and especially equality before and within the law. Indeed, the philosopher Hannah Arendt argues that isonomia is a more apposite name for the Greek polis than democracy, in that it signified no distinction between rulers and ruled. It is little surprise that democracy has always carried subversive undertones: it is the enemy of established hierarchies. Strongmen, then and now, arise to defend hierarchies.

Putin, of course, has a sprawling kleptocracy to defend from the people; he and his cronies did very well out of acquiring old Soviet state-owned assets, and no agitation from the common people will be allowed to disturb the cosy arrangements. Erdoğan, in Turkey, has successfully wound back the Atatürk-inspired secularisation, returning power to the old Ottoman landowners and the conservative clergy. Donald Trump, for his part, is a plutocrat and is determined to ensure that democracy does not threaten plutocratic dominance.

In regard to political leadership, there is little doubt that it is becoming an increasingly difficult task, especially in democracies. Government, as an institution, is everywhere under attack, and public confidence in its capacities is dangerously low. Laura Tingle, in an otherwise perceptive analysis, is mistaken in dismissing "the profound stupidity of the culture wars." Stupid in a sense, yes, but they have provided a platform for a concerted attack on government, which, in a democracy in an increasingly globalised world, is really all that stands between the people and corporate rapacity.

Even before President Ronald Reagan famously labelled government as the problem rather than the solution, a well-funded campaign had been mounted against government, typified by the stated desire of the American libertarian anti-tax campaigner Grover Norquist to reduce government to the size that it could be drowned in a bathtub.

In the United States, the billionaire Koch brothers have funded and assiduously nurtured a right-wing empire of think tanks, foundations, journals and even university schools to denigrate the idea of government. Notably, they have been instrumental in pushing for a reduction of industry regulation across a wide range of fronts – and all this from owners of such environment-polluting assets as oil refineries, pipelines and lumber mills.

At the international level, the whole neoliberal-globalisation project is profoundly anti-democratic. At the end of the Cold War three decades ago, we were assured that free markets would lead to free societies. It was, in the premature triumphalism of Francis Fukuyama, truly the end of history. But, as Robert Reich, prominent US commentator and a member of the Ford, Carter and Clinton administrations, has written, today's supercharged global economy is eroding the power of the people. If neoliberalism has a definable goal, it is to defend capitalism against democracy.

In a 2009 essay entitled "How Capitalism is Killing Democracy," Reich wrote:

> Why has capitalism succeeded while democracy has steadily weakened? Democracy has become enfeebled largely because companies, in intensifying competition for global consumers and investors, have invested ever greater sums in lobbying, public relations, and even bribes and kickbacks, seeking laws that give them a competitive advantage over their rivals. The result is an arms race for political influence that is drowning out the voices of average citizens. In the United States, for example, the fights that preoccupy Congress, those that consume weeks or months of congressional staff time, are typically contests between competing companies or industries.

Political leaders, faced with escalating demands, have been set up to fail. In this pincer movement, global trade agreements hobble governments in their domestic setting on one side, while on the other growing popular revulsion against globalisation opens the door to the shrill voices of anti-democratic demagogues and their movements, along with the rousing of ultra-nationalist sentiments. As Robert Kuttner writes in his new book, *Can Democracy Survive Global Capitalism?*, the rise of terrorism and fear of aliens serves to promote support for anti-foreign strongmen, thus drawing radical Islam and right-wing populism in the West into a bizarre symbiosis.

The eminent Yale historian Timothy Snyder, whose scholarship has illuminated so much of the horrors of interwar Europe and the Holocaust, published a short tract last year, *On Tyranny: Twenty Lessons from the Twentieth Century*, that drew disturbing parallels between the threats to democracy then and now. "We are no wiser than the Europeans who saw democracy yielding to fascism, Nazism, or communism," he wrote. He added: "Our one advantage is that we might learn from their experience."

Just as Lenin was said to have "useful idiots" outside Russia – Western liberals who refused to oppose communism – today's plutocrats have their own useful idiots among the working class and lower-middle classes – those people who have rallied to the populist cause, encouraged to view government as a threat to their status by its giving equal rights to coloured people, immigrants, women, sexual minorities, etc. The force that might rein in corporate dominance and plutocratic control of the economy is now met by a phalanx of opposition from the very people who would benefit most from stronger government.

Historically in Australia, autocratic tendencies have been more in evidence at the state rather than the national level. The bombastic Jack Lang in New South Wales was a home-grown demagogue who almost provoked a coup by the extremist New Guard during the Great Depression. The NSW Liberal premier Bob Askin was no slouch either when it came to blatant populism. Askin, who took some justifiable pride in moving his party towards the centre, exhibited a streak of populism that was, in his latter years, an embarrassment to his supporters. The era that he had dominated was surely over when, during the 1972 federal election campaign, he attacked the ALP for advocating abortion on demand, homosexuality, a "soft approach" to drug offenders and pornographers, and wanting to "flood the country with black people."

Perhaps the closest we have come to an Australian strongman was the long-serving Queensland premier Joh Bjelke-Petersen, who, unconstrained by an upper house and blessed with a feeble Opposition, attacked democratic institutions remorselessly. It was no secret who his enthusiastic backers were: the shonky developers, the tax dodgers, the commercial quacks and so on (the so-called "white-shoe brigade").

So could it happen here? Could Australia fall into the grip of a strongman? The answer, I think, is a cautious no, given the resilience of our institutions – but, nevertheless, we need to be on heightened alert, especially in light of the recent rise of anti-democratic populism. Clearly, there are powerful figures here who would welcome a strongman to do their bidding – in the downfall of Malcolm Turnbull we glimpsed the machinations of billionaires, for some of whom the prospect of a Peter Dutton prime ministership had great appeal. The struggle between democracy, oligarchy and tyranny continues.

Norman Abjorensen

Response to Correspondence

Laura Tingle

Paul Kelly, a great journalistic mentor to me early in my career, would often say, exasperatedly, to the more junior reporters in *The Australian*'s Canberra bureau in the late 1980s and 1990s: "It's the context that's important!"

Context really is everything in political reporting. It is the way of understanding how a political statement or position can remain unchanged, but the movement of everything else around it can leave the statement or position – and the person who holds it – occupying completely different ground to that on which the statement was first made. And of course context, more broadly, means understanding where events or developments fit into a larger story.

Preparing to read through the correspondence on *Follow the Leader*, I reread the last sections of the essay to refresh my mind on where it had ended. You would think that they would be still fairly fresh in my mind, given it is just on two months ago that I was making the last few tweaks to the essay.

Yet the context for doing that was the tumultuous madness of an imploding government terminating yet another Australian prime minister. When you write a book or an essay, you often sneak a look at it a year or two later, hoping that your arguments have withstood the test of time. These days, you wonder whether they have stood the test of even a couple of months.

The point I am getting around to is that rereading the end of the essay made me contemplate how context seems to have disappeared almost completely from our political dialogue. And that has profound implications for our relationships with our leaders, and for our perception of events.

For example, consider the way we viewed the results of the Wentworth by-election pretty much in isolation from many of the political events that preceded it. Sure, there was plenty of discussion of an angry electorate making its feelings known about the toppling of the last prime minister – and the popular local member to boot. There was plenty of discussion, too, of issues such as climate change and asylum seekers. But how much analysis of the historic swing against the Liberal Party was put into the context of what happened just three months earlier, on 28 July, the day of the so-called "Super Saturday" by-elections?

It was noted that the swing in Wentworth was double that in Longman. The result in Longman had, after all, been one of the reasons given for toppling Malcolm Turnbull. But in the Wentworth postmortems, little attention was paid to the outcome as a continuation of what we saw more broadly on 28 July, across five by-elections: a splintering of the major-party vote, and the failure of the major parties to win the centre.

The argument made about Longman was that it was not the size of the swing that was important, but that the LNP's primary vote collapsed to just under 30 per cent. I think that rather misses the point that comes out of both Super Saturday and Wentworth, and which is relevant to my essay.

That obvious point is that, as I said in my essay, the Australian response to disillusionment with politics is overwhelmingly towards disempowering the major parties, rather than looking to a "strongman." I'm sure some voters would still like a strong leader who makes a few sweeping but simple promises about how he or she would make their lives better. But we have had a few of those recently – notably Tony Abbott – and most voters have decided it is not their cup of tea.

The irony here is that, whether in the form of the upset vote for an independent in Wentworth or the now minority status of the Morrison government, voters are stripping the formal leaders of our national politics of their status.

Amanda McKenzie reflects in her response to the essay on the rise of leadership outside formal positions of authority – the sort Ronald Heifetz considers in his book. McKenzie gives the #MeToo movement as an example of this. But it is interesting to consider the extent to which the rise of parliamentary independents is, or becomes, an institutional way to recast the political agenda.

That is, as voters move away from the major parties, and even from minor parties, simple protest votes to reject the current political incumbent may gather enough scale and force to reshape the debate entirely.

To show how tin-eared our professional politicians can be, the prime minister, Scott Morrison, and his colleagues not only disavowed the Wentworth result, but implied that the seat's voters were electoral freaks whose views didn't reflect those of the rest of Australia and, thus, that there was no message to be had from the biggest swing against an incumbent government ever.

All of this gives a little context with which to consider some of the thoughtful contributions made by the correspondents. Katharine Murphy speaks of how politicians need to see themselves – in their positions – as institutional forces, not just players in a drama. And her observations echo those of Sean Kelly, who notes Scott Morrison's dismissive words about not only his new office, but also the institutions that surround it: his own party and both federal–state and international governance.

Morrison has been two months in the job, and the image we have of our latest prime minister is of the ultimate cynic and political apparatchik. If we generously concede that he has little room to manoeuvre because of the imminence of a federal election, we much less generously observe that this did not stop him, nor justify, trashing sensitive and bipartisan policy, and policy-making processes, as he did when publicly raising the question of whether Australia should move its embassy to Jerusalem a week before the Wentworth by-election. This is not leadership. It is not consensus-building. It is not running a calm debate, or consulting with the community.

Senate hearings revealed that this announcement was made without consulting the foreign affairs or defence establishments, without a full and proper cabinet process, and with the foreign minister only finding out about it two days before the announcement.

If you think the prime minister is within his rights to make such a call in such circumstances, you only have to look at what he himself said when he re-adopted the hardest lines on offshore detention – lines softened in the lead-up to the Wentworth by-election. The prime minister was not going to "horse-trade" on this issue, he told a Canberra press conference. He took his advice from the experts on border security matters, not from other politicians. The standing of advice, it appears, varies considerably depending on the subject at hand.

So it seems, under this government at least, that the day-to-day mechanics of leading the country, or showing leadership, have only more sharply deteriorated with a change of prime minister.

But what about the context in which these decisions are made? There is much to be said for Scott Ryan's argument that it is the rise of social issues that previously didn't form part of the domestic political debate that has changed the way our political conversations are conducted.

It is certainly true that it is easier to find compromises or trade-offs on economic issues than it might be on a contentious issue like same-sex marriage, where, as he says, you can legislate or not legislate. But I would argue the change in the way we see our leaders predates the rise of such social issues to the foreground of political contention.

Like Ryan, Nyadol Nyuon considers how the policy context has influenced the conduct of our politics, observing that the War on Terror has transformed Western democracies by expanding what it is acceptable for leaders to do in the domestic sphere.

We should think further about how today's pressing issues have changed and shaped the way we conduct our debates, an idea that, compared with the usual resort to explaining things as an outcome of a faster media cycle, raises interesting questions.

Just as leadership is a two-way relationship between leaders and followers, I'm sure it is true that the scope for leaders to emerge, and the shape of debates that can be had, is driven in part by the nature of the issues we face at any given time. And different subjects also require different tactics.

Political tactics now seem to dominate our leaders' repertoires, yet for all that, these tactics are often simplistic and bombastic. Shireen Morris observes, "The best leaders, when dealing with vexing policy and political problems, take on board the legitimate concerns of their opponents, learn from them and use the lessons to forge a new and better synthesis position. They hammer out a noble compromise." Her observation reminded me that some of our more cunning political leaders of recent decades were experts in the art of stealing their opponent's policy clothes, but wrapping them up in their own decoration, in a way that made it hard for the other side to oppose a policy. Since it generally feels that our leaders these days start from the point of assessed political advantage, rather than policy principle, it is difficult to see how they can then adapt such fleet-of-foot tactics.

Discussing *Follow the Leader* in many forums and interviews in the last couple of months has only confirmed to me the deep pessimism many Australians have about the state of our political leadership. Strangely, having thought about it so intensively in the last year, and having to observe the paucity of it in my day job over the past few decades, I am not as pessimistic as many others. We should not despair and believe it is impossible for our leadership to get better, or that the modern news cycle makes it impossible. I look at leaders like Jacinda Ardern in New Zealand, and what Angela Merkel was able to achieve over two extraordinary decades in Germany's history, and am reminded that periodically, often when you least expect it, someone does come along with a particular set of talents and finds themselves in a context where they can change the political conversation. They can speak intelligently to the electorate. They offer substance, not slogans.

The institutions of our political leadership may be on the wane and being transformed by disillusioned voters. But that does not mean good political leadership is a thing of the past.

Laura Tingle

Norman Abjorensen is a political historian. He works on the global evaluation project Varieties of Democracy at the University of Gothenburg, Sweden, and is co-author of *Australia: The State of Democracy* and the *Historical Dictionary of Australia*. His history of democracy will be published next year.

Dennis Atkins is *The Courier-Mail*'s national affairs editor and the writer of its "Party Games" column. He has a regular spot on ABC TV's *Insiders*.

Sean Kelly is a columnist for Fairfax, a contributor to *The Saturday Paper* and *The Monthly*, and a former adviser to prime ministers Kevin Rudd and Julia Gillard.

Amanda McKenzie is CEO of the Climate Council and was a founder of the Australian Youth Climate Coalition.

Shireen Morris is the Labor candidate for the seat of Deakin. She is the author of *Radical Heart* and the editor of *A Rightful Place* and co-editor of *The Forgotten People*.

Katharine Murphy is *Guardian Australia*'s political editor. She won the Paul Lyneham Award for press gallery journalism in 2008, and was a Walkley award finalist for digital journalism in 2012. She is the author of *On Disruption*.

Nyadol Nyuon is a lawyer at Arnold Bloch Leibler, a writer and a community advocate.

Scott Ryan is a Liberal senator for Victoria. He has been the President of the Senate since November 2017.

Sebastian Smee is the author of *The Art of Rivalry* and art critic for *The Washington Post*. He won the Pulitzer Prize for Criticism in 2011 and was a runner-up in 2008. His writing has appeared in *The Boston Globe*, *The Australian*, *The Sydney Morning Herald*, *The Monthly*, *The Guardian*, *The Independent*, *The Times*, *The Financial Times* and *The Spectator*.

Laura Tingle is chief political correspondent for ABC TV's *7.30*. She won the Paul Lyneham Award for press gallery journalism in 2004 and Walkley awards in 2005 and 2011. She is the author of *Chasing the Future: Recession, Recovery and the New Politics in Australia* and three acclaimed Quarterly Essays, *Great Expectations*, *Political Amnesia* and *Follow the Leader*.

QUARTERLY ESSAY BACK ISSUES

BACK ISSUES: (Prices include GST, postage and handling within Australia.)

- ☐ **QE 1** ($15.99) Robert Manne *In Denial*
- ☐ **QE 2** ($15.99) John Birmingham *Appeasing Jakarta*
- ☐ **QE 3** ($15.99) Guy Rundle *The Opportunist*
- ☐ **QE 4** ($15.99) Don Watson *Rabbit Syndrome*
- ☐ **QE 5** ($15.99) Mungo MacCallum *Girt By Sea*
- ☐ **QE 6** ($15.99) John Button *Beyond Belief*
- ☐ **QE 7** ($15.99) John Martinkus *Paradise Betrayed*
- ☐ **QE 8** ($15.99) Amanda Lohrey *Groundswell*
- ☐ **QE 9** ($15.99) Tim Flannery *Beautiful Lies*
- ☐ **QE 10** ($15.99) Gideon Haigh *Bad Company*
- ☐ **QE 11** ($15.99) Germaine Greer *Whitefella Jump Up*
- ☐ **QE 12** ($15.99) David Malouf *Made in England*
- ☐ **QE 13** ($15.99) Robert Manne with David Corlett *Sending Them Home*
- ☐ **QE 14** ($15.99) Paul McGeough *Mission Impossible*
- ☐ **QE 15** ($15.99) Margaret Simons *Latham's World*
- ☐ **QE 16** ($15.99) Raimond Gaita *Breach of Trust*
- ☐ **QE 17** ($15.99) John Hirst *'Kangaroo Court'*
- ☐ **QE 18** ($15.99) Gail Bell *The Worried Well*
- ☐ **QE 19** ($15.99) Judith Brett *Relaxed & Comfortable*
- ☐ **QE 20** ($15.99) John Birmingham *A Time for War*
- ☐ **QE 21** ($15.99) Clive Hamilton *What's Left?*
- ☐ **QE 22** ($15.99) Amanda Lohrey *Voting for Jesus*
- ☐ **QE 23** ($15.99) Inga Clendinnen *The History Question*
- ☐ **QE 24** ($15.99) Robyn Davidson *No Fixed Address*
- ☐ **QE 25** ($15.99) Peter Hartcher *Bipolar Nation*
- ☐ **QE 26** ($15.99) David Marr *His Master's Voice*
- ☐ **QE 27** ($15.99) Ian Lowe *Reaction Time*
- ☐ **QE 28** ($15.99) Judith Brett *Exit Right*
- ☐ **QE 29** ($15.99) Anne Manne *Love & Money*
- ☐ **QE 30** ($15.99) Paul Toohey *Last Drinks*
- ☐ **QE 31** ($15.99) Tim Flannery *Now or Never*
- ☐ **QE 32** ($15.99) Kate Jennings *American Revolution*
- ☐ **QE 33** ($15.99) Guy Pearse *Quarry Vision*
- ☐ **QE 34** ($15.99) Annabel Crabb *Stop at Nothing*
- ☐ **QE 35** ($15.99) Noel Pearson *Radical Hope*
- ☐ **QE 36** ($15.99) Mungo MacCallum *Australian Story*
- ☐ **QE 37** ($15.99) Waleed Aly *What's Right?*
- ☐ **QE 38** ($15.99) David Marr *Power Trip*
- ☐ **QE 39** ($15.99) Hugh White *Power Shift*
- ☐ **QE 40** ($15.99) George Megalogenis *Trivial Pursuit*
- ☐ **QE 41** ($15.99) David Malouf *The Happy Life*
- ☐ **QE 42** ($15.99) Judith Brett *Fair Share*
- ☐ **QE 43** ($15.99) Robert Manne *Bad News*
- ☐ **QE 44** ($15.99) Andrew Charlton *Man-Made World*
- ☐ **QE 45** ($15.99) Anna Krien *Us and Them*
- ☐ **QE 46** ($15.99) Laura Tingle *Great Expectations*
- ☐ **QE 47** ($15.99) David Marr *Political Animal*
- ☐ **QE 48** ($15.99) Tim Flannery *After the Future*
- ☐ **QE 49** ($15.99) Mark Latham *Not Dead Yet*
- ☐ **QE 50** ($15.99) Anna Goldsworthy *Unfinished Business*
- ☐ **QE 51** ($15.99) David Marr *The Prince*
- ☐ **QE 52** ($15.99) Linda Jaivin *Found in Translation*
- ☐ **QE 53** ($15.99) Paul Toohey *That Sinking Feeling*
- ☐ **QE 54** ($15.99) Andrew Charlton *Dragon's Tail*
- ☐ **QE 55** ($15.99) Noel Pearson *A Rightful Place*
- ☐ **QE 56** ($15.99) Guy Rundle *Clivosaurus*
- ☐ **QE 57** ($15.99) Karen Hitchcock *Dear Life*
- ☐ **QE 58** ($15.99) David Kilcullen *Blood Year*
- ☐ **QE 59** ($15.99) David Marr *Faction Man*
- ☐ **QE 60** ($15.99) Laura Tingle *Political Amnesia*
- ☐ **QE 61** ($15.99) George Megalogenis *Balancing Act*
- ☐ **QE 62** ($15.99) James Brown *Firing Line*
- ☐ **QE 63** ($15.99) Don Watson *Enemy Within*
- ☐ **QE 64** ($15.99) Stan Grant *The Australian Dream*
- ☐ **QE 65** ($15.99) David Marr *The White Queen*
- ☐ **QE 66** ($15.99) Anna Krien *The Long Goodbye*
- ☐ **QE 67** ($15.99) Benjamin Law *Moral Panic 101*
- ☐ **QE 68** ($22.99) Hugh White *Without America*
- ☐ **QE 69** ($22.99) Mark McKenna *Moment of Truth*
- ☐ **QE 70** ($22.99) Richard Denniss *Dead Right*
- ☐ **QE 71** ($22.99) Laura Tingle *Follow the Leader*

NAME:

ADDRESS:

EMAIL: PHONE:

Please include this form with payment details on the opposite page.